pathfinder guide

Cotswold

WALKS

Compiled by
John Brooks and
Brian Conduit

D0050430

Acknowledgements
We would like to thank Mr B.E. Fryer of the Cotswold
Voluntary Warden Service; Mrs G. Pietrzak, Principal Rights
of Way Officer, Oxfordshire County Council; and Ms F.H.
Crann of the National Trust (Severn Regional Office), for
looking at the manuscript and giving us much useful advice.

Text:	Brian Conduit, John Brooks
Photography:	John Brooks, Jarrold Publishing
Editors:	Thomas Albrighton, Donald Greig
Designers:	Brian Skinner, Doug Whitworth
Mapping:	Heather Pearson, Sandy Sims

Series Consultant: Brian Conduit

Jarrold Publishing   ISBN 0-7117-0458-9

While every care has been taken to ensure the accuracy of the
route directions, the publishers cannot accept responsibility
for errors or omissions, or for changes in details given. The
countryside is not static: hedges and fences can be removed,
field boundaries can alter, footpaths can be rerouted and
changes in ownership can result in the closure or diversion of
some concessionary paths. Also, paths that are easy and
pleasant for walking in fine conditions may become slippery,
muddy and difficult in wet weather, while stepping stones
across rivers and streams may become impassable.
   If you find an inaccuracy in either the text or maps, please
write to Jarrold Publishing or Ordnance Survey respectively at
one of the addresses below.

First published 1990
by Jarrold Publishing and Ordnance Survey
Reprinted 1991, 1993, 1996, 1998

Printed in Great Britain
by Jarrold Book Printing, Thetford 5/98

Jarrold Publishing,
Whitefriars, Norwich NR3 1TR
Ordnance Survey,
Romsey Road, Southampton SO16 4GU

Front cover:	Northleach
Previous page:	Chipping Campden

Contents

Short, easy walks

Walks of modest length, likely to involve some modest uphill walking

More challenging walks which may be longer and/or over more rugged terrain, often with some stiff climbs

Keymap 1

SCALE 1:250 000 or 1 INCH to 4 MILES *1CM to 2.5KM*

Keymap 1

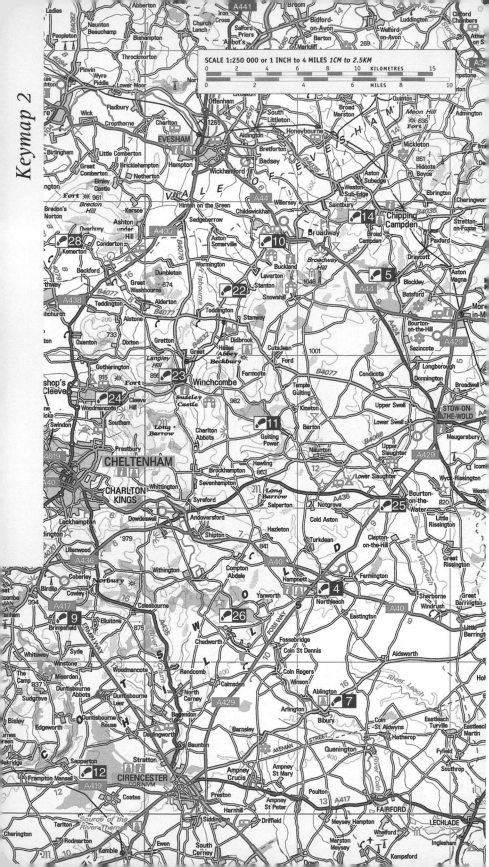

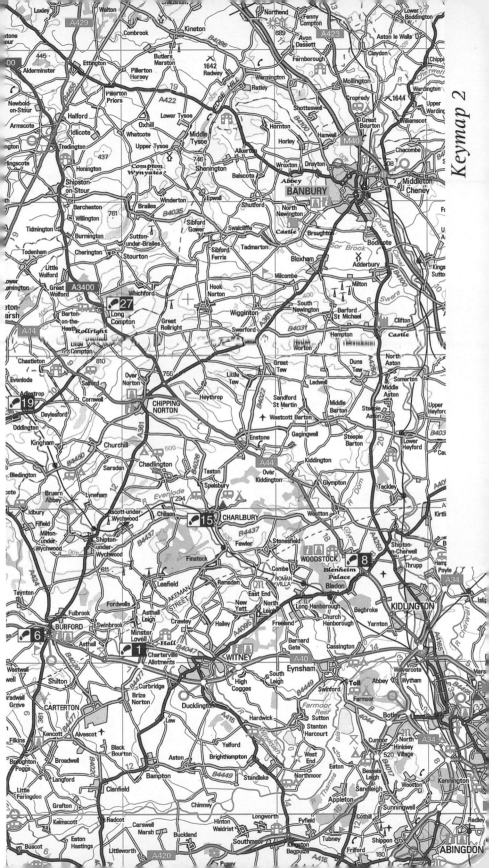

Keymap 2

At-a-glance...

Walk	Page	Start	Distance	Time
Adlestrop, Cornwell and Oddington	56	Adlestrop	8 miles (12.75km)	4 hrs
Bath and Claverton Down	60	Bath	8½ miles (13.5km)	4 hrs
Bibury and the River Coln	26	Bibury	6 miles (9.5km)	3 hrs
Blenheim Park	29	Woodstock	6½ miles (10.5km)	3½ hrs
Blockley and Norcombe Wood	22	Blockley	4½ miles (7.25km)	2½ hrs
Bourton-on-the-Water, the Slaughters and Naunton	75	Bourton-on-the-Water	10 miles (16km)	5 hrs
Bredon Hill	86	Overbury	9½ miles (15.25km)	5 hrs
Brimpsfield and Syde	32	Brimpsfield	6½ miles (10.5km)	3½ hrs
Broadway and Broadway Tower	34	Broadway	4 miles (6.5km)	2 hrs
Burford, Fulbrook and Widford	24	Burford	5½ miles (8.75km)	2½ hrs
Castle Combe	16	Castle Combe	4 miles (6.5km)	2 hrs
Chedworth and Withington	79	Chedworth	9 miles (14.5km)	5 hrs
Chipping Campden and Dover's Hill	44	Chipping Campden	5 miles (8km)	2½ hrs
Cleeve Common	72	Cleeve Common	8 miles (12.75km)	4 hrs
Cooper's Hill and Buckholt Wood	48	Cooper's Hill	5½ miles (8.75km)	3 hrs
Dyrham Park and West Littleton	42	Off the A46, south of M4 Junction 18	5½ miles (8.75km)	3 hrs
The Guitings and Guiting Wood	37	Kineton	6½ miles (10.5km)	3 hrs
Haresfield Beacon and Standish Wood	53	Shortwood	7 miles (11.25km)	3½ hrs
Laurie Lee Country	62	Slad	7 miles (11.25km)	4½ hrs
Minchinhampton Common	18	Minchinhampton	4½ miles (7.25km)	2 hrs
Minster Lovell and the River Windrush	14	Minster Lovell	3½ miles (5.5km)	2 hrs
Northleach and Hampnett	20	Northleach	4 miles (6.5km)	2 hrs
The Rollright Stones	83	Long Compton	9 miles (14.5km)	4½ hrs
Sapperton and Daneway	40	Sapperton	4½ miles (7.25km)	3 hrs
Stanton, Stanway and Snowshill	65	Stanton	8 miles (12.75km)	5½ hrs
Winchcombe, Hailes Abbey and Sudeley Castle	68	Winchcombe	8½ miles (13.5km)	4½ hrs
Wotton-under-Edge, the Tyndale Monument and Coombe Hill	50	Wotton-under-Edge	5½ miles (8.75km)	3½ hrs
Wychwood Forest	46	Charlbury	7 miles (11.25km)	4 hrs

Comments

A number of idyllic villages with interesting churches are passed on this walk in the lovely Evenlode valley, and there is also the opportunity to visit a 17th-century mansion.

Follow the Kennet and Avon Canal as it curves around the northern and easten fringes of Bath, finishing with a magnificent view over this elegant city.

Two attractive villages are linked by this walk through woodland and across meadows by the banks of the placid River Coln.

A walk through landscaped parkland and near the end you enjoy tremendous views of Blenheim Palace across the lake.

Enticing field and woodland paths radiate from the village of Blockley.

One of the classic walks of the Cotswolds that visits four outstandingly attractive and varied villages in the lovely Windrush valley.

A long walk, but the climb over Bredon Hill is neither difficult nor steep and the magnificent views more than compensate for the effort.

Much of this route follows woodland paths, best in spring or autumn but possibly muddy after prolonged rain. The gradients are undemanding, though there is a climb if you take the detour to Syde church.

A climb to one of the finest viewpoints in the Cotswolds is followed by a descent into one of the region's most popular villages.

The outward section of this gentle walk is largely on field paths while the return is through riverside meadows. The setting of the church in the lost village of Widford is particularly memorable.

Judge for yourself whether Castle Combe is the prettiest village in England, as is often alleged

Some superb woodland and two interesting villages are passed through, and there is the chance to visit one of the best-preserved Roman villas in the country.

From one of the finest of Cotswold wool towns, you emerge on to the escarpment to enjoy extensive views across the Vale of Evesham.

Superb views are enjoyed as you walk over one of the few surviving areas of open common to the highest point in the Cotswolds, and also pass a prehistoric burial chamber.

Much of this walk is through beautiful beech woodland and there are also fine views across the Vale of Severn.

The southern Cotswolds provide viewpoints over large tracts of countryside. The walk allows you to enjoy views towards Bristol and the River Severn as well as taking you past a notable mansion and deer park.

This walk passes through Guiting Wood, one of the largest expanses of unspoilt woodland in the Cotswolds. The route also leads through fields and along quiet lanes and visits three lovely villages.

There is an element of cheating in this walk as it begins on the crest of the western Cotswolds at Haresfield Beacon, later descending from Scottsquar Hill to Randwick before climbing back to the ridge.

Laurie Lee's account of his early life in the Cotswolds, *Cider with Rosie*, has become a classic, and it attracts many people to the village of Syde where he grew up.

From the elevated Minchinhampton Common there are grand views over the Nailsworth and Frome valleys.

The combination of medieval church and ruined hall above the water meadows of the Windrush is an unforgettable sight.

This route makes an enjoyable stroll in the valley of the little River Leach. Be sure to visit the wonderful church at Northleach, one of the grandest of the Cotswold wool churches.

Centrepiece of this walk is a group of prehistoric remains situated on a ridge, from which there are superb and extensive views.

This is one of the few walks in this book which fails to include a notable viewpoint. In spite of this it makes an interesting outing and has variety as well as historical interest.

The strenuous part of this walk comes near the half-way point with the climb through Lidcombe Wood. The route also passes through fields, parkland and two delightful villages – Stanway and Snowshill.

Plenty of variety in this walk that starts in a typical Cotswold wool town and includes a ruined Cistercian abbey and a 15th-century manor house.

Nibley Knoll and Coombe Hill are two summits on the western flanks of the Cotswolds, both excellent viewpoints. The hardest climb comes early on and Coombe Hill is a fitting finale to an excellent route.

This walk takes you through the quiet woodlands and glades of a former royal hunting ground.

At-a-glance...

Introduction to the Cotswolds

Nowhere else in the country do the work of nature and the work of man appear to be in greater harmony than in the Cotswolds. There are other parts of England that possess more dramatic scenery and there are equally attractive villages in other regions, but here is a combination of idyllic stone villages and small towns set amidst a gentle, rolling countryside that is without parallel and quintessentially 'English'.

How has this uniquely attractive combination been created and largely preserved? To explain this we need to examine three major factors relating to the geology, history and geography of the region: the local stone, the development of the woollen industry and the lack of nearby coal deposits.

Local Stone

The Cotswolds form part of a line of uplands, composed of oolitic limestone, that stretches in a roughly north-east to south-west direction from Yorkshire to Dorset. *Wold* is a Saxon word meaning 'upland'; the origin of *cot* is more difficult to establish. One theory is that it comes from the Saxon word for sheep enclosure; an alternative suggestion is that it is derived from *Cod*, the name of a Saxon chief who settled in the upper Windrush valley. Possibly the name Cotswold originally may have referred only to the area around the Windrush, later extended to cover the whole of this upland region.

Unlike the carboniferous limestone of the Yorkshire Dales and the Mendips, oolitic limestone does not create deep gorges and underground cave systems but a more intimate and less dramatic landscape characterised by rolling hills and gentle valleys. The Cotswolds tilt slightly to the south-east, thereby thrusting up a bold and often steep escarpment on their western edge. From this escarpment a succession of fine viewpoints – Dover's Hill, Broadway Tower, Cleeve Common, Cooper's Hill, Haresfield Beacon, Wotton Hill and Hinton Hill – look westwards over the lowlands of the vales of Evesham, Gloucester, and Berkeley to the equally bold outlines of the Malverns, Shropshire Hills and Black Mountains on the distant horizon. Nearer at hand the eye is drawn to a number of individual outlying hills detached from the main Cotswold range; two of the most prominent of these are Bredon Hill near Evesham and Robins Wood Hill overlooking Gloucester.

Behind the escarpment lies the long 'dip' slope. Here is the typical rolling wold country which drops gently to the formerly extensive royal hunting ground of Wychwood Forest and merges almost imperceptibly into the flat country of the Oxford Plain. In the north of the region a number of rivers with delightful-sounding names – Evenlode, Windrush, Leach, Coln – have cut wide valleys through the wolds, flowing south-eastwards into the plain eventually to join the Thames, a Cotswold river in its origin. Only in the south, in the narrower valleys around Stroud, do the rivers flow westwards to the Severn. Uniquely among Cotswold rivers, the Bristol Avon describes a great arc, flowing first eastwards, then turning southwards and finally curving westwards through Bradford-on-Avon and on to Bath, to form an obvious southern boundary to the Cotswolds. The northern edge is less clearly defined but here the line of limestone uplands descends to the valley of another River Avon, the Warwickshire or Shakespeare's Avon.

Cotswold stone makes excellent building material and has been used extensively for this purpose. One of its most appealing features is the

variation in colour shades which can range, depending on area, from light grey through pale cream, yellow, honey and deep golden to light brown. It is above all the quality and colour of this limestone, which invariably looks warm on even the dullest day, which makes the villages and

Keble's Bridge, Eastleach

small towns of the region so attractive. So well do some of the smaller villages blend into their natural surroundings that they seem to be an integral part of the landscape.

Woollen Industry

In his *Britannia*, published in 1610, William Camden says of the Cotswolds, 'In these Woulds there feed, in great numbers, flockes of sheepe'. If the local limestone produced the basic material for the buildings of the region, it was the prosperity generated initially by these 'flockes of sheepe' that provided the money for them. Much of the rich architectural heritage of the Cotswolds comes from the development of the medieval wool trade.

Sheep farming began with the first human inhabitants of the region. With their dry slopes and sheltered valleys, the Cotswolds were a popular area for settlement from earliest times and a large number of varied prehistoric monuments survive. Among the best-known and most impressive of these are the burial chamber at Belas Knap, the group of remains known collectively as the Rollright Stones, and the Iron Age fortifications which made use of the high vantage points. The summits of

Bredon Hill, Cleeve Hill and Haresfield Beacon are among many that are crowned with such defensive earthworks but the most elaborate and extensive are those that occupy the plateau of Minchinhampton Common above the Frome and Nailsworth valleys.

The Romans found the area congenial and relatively easy to penetrate. They established Corinium (Cirencester) as one of their principal cities and Aquae Sulis (Bath) as their major health resort, building a number of villas, for example at Chedworth and Witcombe, and constructing a series of roads – Foss Way, Ermin Street, Akeman Street – across the region. After the Romans came the Anglo-Saxons, who founded most of the present-day settlements and later introduced Christianity into the area. Last in the line of conquerors were the Normans who in the years after 1066 rebuilt many

The main street at Burford

of the churches, established strong castles on the fringes of the region at Oxford and Gloucester and also created the royal forest of Wychwood which lies around Burford, Charlbury and Woodstock.

It was the monastic foundations of the Cotswolds (Cirencester, Winchcombe, Hailes) that helped to pioneer the development of the wool trade which reached its peak between the 14th and 17th centuries. At first the raw wool was exported to the continent but in the early 14th century Edward III imported weavers from Flanders to develop a native cloth industry. Over the next few centuries the manufacturing of woollen cloth expanded and prospered and by the end of the Middle Ages it had become England's major export industry. Half of it was produced in the Cotswolds, where the advantages of an abundance of sheep, water power and good communications ensured the predominance of the region.

It is from this heyday of the cloth trade that the distinguished architectural legacy of the area – domestic, commercial and religious – chiefly dates. This includes comparatively humble buildings, like small village churches, farmhouses, market halls and the modest but dignified houses and cottages that adorn such delightful places as Castle Combe, Bourton-on-the-Water and Bibury, as well as the grander town houses of wool merchants and the manor houses at Minster Lovell, Snowshill and Chastleton. Particularly outstanding are the magnificent 15th-century 'wool churches', endowed by wealthy wool magnates like William Grevel of Chipping Campden and the Forteys of Northleach. All visitors will have their favourites, but probably the most impressive are those that rise above Cirencester, Winchcombe, Burford, Chipping Campden and Northleach.

Lack of Coal

It is fortunate that much of this rich legacy has survived relatively intact and unspoilt and this is largely due to the absence of local coal deposits. With the onset of the Industrial Revolution, and in particular the application of first water- and later steam-powered machinery, the Cotswold woollen industry declined, unable to compete with the textile areas on the slopes of the Pennines which had the advantages of faster flowing streams and proximity to coal. Only the area around Stroud, where the streams are fast flowing, was able to expand and prolong its status as an important cloth producing region into the early 19th century, until it also lost out to the more powerful woollen industries of Yorkshire. Here the narrow valleys, with their steep sides covered in tiers of houses and with 19th-century mills in the valley bottoms, rather resemble the Pennine valleys of Lancashire and Yorkshire – except that they never became extensively urbanised and industrialised.

Throughout the region the decline of the woollen industry led to much hardship and poverty – it is difficult to conceive of such an obviously prosperous area as this ever suffering hardship – but paradoxically it was this that was largely instrumental in preserving the attractiveness of the Cotswolds. Relative economic stagnation prevented the large-scale rebuilding, urbanisation and inevitable environmental damage that scarred so many other parts of Britain during the era of the Industrial Revolution.

In time a regeneration took place, largely based on the permanent advantages of the region – its climate, countryside and accessibility – that made it an attractive place to live and later a popular tourist area. A number of great country houses were built during the 18th and 19th centuries, including Cornbury Park, Blenheim Palace and Sezincote. In the late Georgian and Regency periods Cheltenham prospered and expanded as a fashionable spa and residential town. William Morris, the influential Victorian arbiter of taste and social reformer, helped to start off the tourist industry by popularising such beauty spots as Bibury and Broadway. During the 20th century the car has opened up the whole area to many more visitors and now tourism has become a vital part of the economy of the Cotswolds.

In Shakespeare's *Richard II* the Cotswolds are described as 'high wild hills and rough uneven ways', but in the main this is no longer true. Apart from a few remaining unenclosed 'wild' areas such as Cleeve Common, this is an intimate and largely tamed landscape where the man-made features of churches, villages, farms and manor houses fit snugly into their physical surroundings of hills and valleys, fields and woodlands. By far the best way to explore and appreciate at first hand this uniquely beautiful and harmonious corner of England is on foot and an extensive network of waymarked paths enables you to do that – an immensely rewarding and pleasurable experience.

Minster Lovell and the River Windrush

Start	Minster Lovell
Distance	3½ miles (5.5km)
Approximate time	2 hours
Parking	Minster Lovell
Refreshments	Pub at Minster Lovell, pub at Crawley
Ordnance Survey maps	Landranger 164 (Oxford) and Pathfinder 1091, SP 21/31 (Burford & Witney (North))

This is a relaxing half-day stroll amidst the gentle scenery of the Windrush valley which lies between the exceptionally interesting village of Minster Lovell and Witney. The first part of the route across the water meadows by the river is delightful. Then the route heads across to the village of Crawley, returning to Minster Lovell along the edge of the valley from where there are some fine views.

The walk begins at the car park by the bridge over the Windrush. Follow the direction of a 'Circular Walk' footpath sign across a recreation ground to climb a yellow-waymarked stile in the far left-hand corner. Continue along the left-hand edge of a meadow and soon there is a fine view of the church and hall in front; climb a stile in the wire fence on the left and follow the path towards the church. Climb another stile to enter the churchyard and walk between the church and highly atmospheric ruins of Minster Lovell Hall, following blue waymarks round to the right to a kissing-gate and public footpath sign.

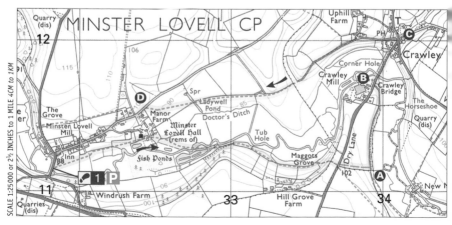

The combination of church and hall occupying a lovely position above the banks of the placid Windrush could hardly be more picturesque or typically English, especially when the church tower is viewed between the jagged walls of the ruined hall. The cruciform church, unusually imposing for a small village, was initially part of a priory which was a daughter house of an abbey in Normandy.

The ruined Manor House at Minster Lovell

In the Hundred Years War with France, these so-called 'alien priories' were regarded as enemy property and in 1414 were confiscated by Henry V. The church then reverted to a conventional parish church. Both church and hall date from the 15th century, the result of a rebuilding programme carried out by William Lovell, lord of the manor. The hall was rectangular and fortified, a sign of the troubled times in which it was built. Since being dismantled in 1747 it has steadily fallen into ruin, but its ruinous state only enhances the romance and air of mystery surrounding the place.

Turn left through the kissing-gate, cross a yellow-waymarked footbridge a few yards ahead and continue across flat meadowland to another footbridge, this time over the River Windrush. Cross it and keep to a path that bears left by the river and through trees to a stile. Climb over and continue over a series of stiles, eventually entering thick woodland through which the path climbs to a stile at the far end. Climb over, continue across the field ahead, with fine and expansive views in front, to climb another stile and continue on to a lane. Cross over, squeeze through a gap by the side of a metal gate opposite and continue along the edge of the next field, with a hedge on the left, heading downhill to a gate on the right **Ⓐ**.

Do not go through the gate but instead turn left, pass through another gate a few yards ahead and continue, between trees and a wire fence on the left and trees and a ditch on the right, up to a metal gate **Ⓑ**. Go through this on to the road opposite Crawley Mill and turn right over the bridge and into Crawley village.

In the village centre turn left opposite the War Memorial **Ⓒ** along Farm Lane, passing the Lamb Inn on the right. Continue along this lane which climbs gently above the Windrush valley, with a good view of Crawley Mill below to the left. Just by the first cottages on the right, where the lane bends to the right, bear left, at a footpath sign to Minster Lovell, along a broad, clearly defined, hedge-lined path. Gaps in the trees and hedges on the left reveal attractive views over the valley. Emerging from the confines of the trees and hedges, keep ahead a few yards, climb a fence and walk along the right-hand edge of a field, by a wall on the right. Climb a stone stile, continue along the edge of the next field – Minster Lovell church tower and the ruins of the hall can soon be seen ahead – to climb another stile at the far end of the field. Now turn half-right and go diagonally across the next field to a stile in the far right-hand corner.

Climb over and turn left **Ⓓ** along the lane into Minster Lovell, continuing down the village street which is lined by stone and thatched cottages, to the Old Swan Inn at the bottom. Here turn left back to the bridge and car park. ●

Castle Combe

Start	Castle Combe
Distance	4 miles (6.5km)
Approximate time	2 hours
Parking	Car park ½ mile (800m) north of Castle Combe
Refreshments	Pubs and tea-rooms at Castle Combe
Ordnance Survey maps	Landranger 173 (Swindon & Devizes) and Pathfinder 1168, ST 87/97 (Chippenham & Castle Combe)

On their far south-eastern fringes the Cotswolds overlap into Wiltshire and in this region there are some attractive villages set in a gentle wooded landscape. The picture-postcard village of Castle Combe, in the valley of By Brook, is the best-known and most visited of these and forms a focal point of a leisurely half-day stroll, ideal when the weather is not so good, or when time is short, or when you simply want some pleasant, modest exercise.

Turn right out of the car park down a tree-lined lane to a T-junction where you turn right again. Where the road starts to bear left downhill bear slightly right **Ⓐ** along a tarmac track, at a footpath sign to Nettleton Shrub, passing cottages and a school on the right and continuing between stone gateposts to a stile. Climb over and walk along the left-hand edge of a field to climb a stile at the far end, continuing downhill into the trees to a footpath sign at a path junction. Turn left, climb a stile and head downhill along a path enclosed by walls. Go under a bridge, bending sharp left and following a tarmac drive under an arch into Castle Combe opposite the church.

Castle Combe is in the same league as Broadway, Bourton-on-the-Water and Bibury, regarded by many as not only the finest village in the Cotswolds but even as the prettiest in England. Dignified, golden-coloured stone

cottages, mainly 17th- and 18th-century, lie in a sheltered wooded valley through which flows By Brook crossed by graceful old bridges; a market cross stands in the village centre, inns and tea shops cater for the many visitors, and presiding over this scene is the fine medieval church. Nothing looks untidy or out of place and it is not surprising that the village has been used on occasions as a film location. As in the rest of the Cotswolds, wool was the basis of Castle Combe's prosperity. In the woods to the north are the earthworks of the Norman motte and bailey castle from which the village gets its name.

Turn left for a few yards up to the market cross where you turn right **Ⓑ** and continue through the village. Cross a bridge over By Brook and keep ahead by the brook on the left, shortly recrossing it **Ⓒ**. On the other side of the footbridge turn right at a footpath

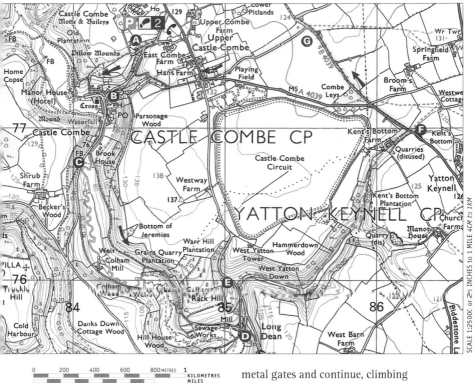

SCALE 1:25000 or 2½ INCHES to 1 MILE 4CM to 1KM

sign to Long Dean, climb a stile and
continue along the side of the well-
wooded valley above By Brook, by a
wire fence on the right. Climb a stone
stile – the area between the first and
second stiles is a nature reserve – and
head gently downhill to join a rough
track, which you follow past a former
mill on the right to a lane **D**.

Turn left up to a T-junction, where
you climb a stile immediately ahead **E**,
to the right of a metal gate. Now turn
left along a path that runs parallel to
the road for a few yards before bearing
right through a valley, by a line of trees
on the right, climbing very gradually
and passing through a metal gate.
Continue through Hammerdown Wood,
go through a gate at the far end and
follow a rather indistinct path across
rough grassland along the bottom of
the tree-lined valley. Go through two

metal gates and continue, climbing
gently to pass through another gate. At
this stage sounds of racing cars may be
heard as the Castle Combe circuit is just
over to the left. Continue past a farm
on the left, on through a metal gate and
along the farm drive to a road **F**.

Turn left for ¼ mile (400m) and
where the road bends to the left keep
ahead, by a byway sign, along a
wooded bridleway, later continuing
past a house on the right to a lane **G**.
Turn left along this narrow lane for
½ mile (800m) to a T-junction, turning
right to another junction a few yards
ahead and then continuing straight
ahead, at a footpath sign to Castle
Combe, along a tarmac track. Where
that track ends, bear slightly right
along a tree-lined path which heads
gently downhill and, ignoring paths to
the left, continue down to a road. Turn
right uphill, bearing left at the first
junction, signposted to Acton Turville,
back to the car park. ●

Minchinhampton Common

Start	Minchinhampton
Distance	4½ miles (7.25km)
Approximate time	2 hours
Parking	Minchinhampton
Refreshments	Pubs and cafés at Minchinhampton, Old Lodge Inn on Minchinhampton Common
Ordnance Survey maps	Landranger 162 (Gloucester & Forest of Dean) and Pathfinder 1113, SO 80/90 (Stroud)

The National Trust property of Minchinhampton Common is one of the largest areas of remaining open common land in the Cotswolds, occupying a plateau above the steep-sided and tightly packed Frome and Nailsworth valleys to the south-east of Stroud. The advantages of its location are obvious: flat, easy walking with fine views across the valleys for very little effort. The common is criss-crossed by public footpaths, but many of these are not visible on the ground and in any case they are largely unnecessary – walkers can wander freely and there are plenty of landmarks to make trouble-free route finding.

Minchinhampton is a charming little wool town with narrow streets converging on the lovely old Market Square. Here the main focal point is the attractive 17th-century Market House, and a few yards away along Bell Street is the unusually imposing cruciform church which has an almost cathedral-like appearance, apart from its distinctive truncated spire. It dates from the 12th century and has a fine aisled nave and a superb rose window in the ornate south transept. Much of Minchinhampton's quiet, rather old-fashioned charm stems from the fact that 19th-century development of the local cloth industry took place down in the valleys, where there was water to power the mills, leaving the town literally high and dry as a monument to the earlier phase of that industry.

Start in the Market Square and walk along Bell Lane to the left of the church, following the churchyard wall to the right and up on to the common. Turn left **Ⓐ** along the edge of the common, at first along a tarmac drive and later across grass, keeping all the while by the boundary wall of houses on the left, to a road. Cross the road and continue ahead, still by a wall on the left. The prominent embankment on the right is part of extensive Iron Age defences called The Bulwarks. After the wall on the left ends, keep ahead towards the right-hand edge of the trees in front, cross another road **Ⓑ** and continue, again by a wall on the left. Where that wall bends to the left, turn half-left and head across the common to pass through the Iron Age embankment and on to the road beyond. Cross it and continue over the open common towards the enclosure

The market square at Minchinhampton

and buildings slightly to the right, the latter being a golf club and a pub.

Taking care to dodge golf balls, continue beyond the pub, heading in the direction of the houses of Amberley in front. Cross the road, just to the right of a sharp bend, and continue towards the right-hand side of the houses, making for a war memorial when you see it **C**. From here there is a superb view ahead over the Frome valley. Do not cross the road to the memorial but turn right, at first by the garden walls of the houses on the left and later continuing in a straight line to a road. Cross over, turn half-right and head across to a group of houses and trees in front, which mark the edge of Burleigh.

On reaching the road turn left along it for about 100 yds (92m) and opposite a bus shelter bear right **D** along a narrow lane and follow it for nearly ¹⁄₂ mile (800m) to a road. The views over the Frome valley to the left are outstanding. At the road bear left and where it bends to the left over a cattle-grid, keep ahead along another narrow, curving lane for ¹⁄₂ mile (800m), bearing left at the next junction. Where the lane curves to the left continue, by a National Trust sign to Besbury Common, along a path by the edge of the common, keeping by a wall on the right. Go through two squeezer stiles and just before a third one turn right **E** through another and keep along the right-hand edge of a field, by a wire fence on the right, up to a stile. Climb it, cross a farm drive, climb a stone stile ahead and continue, climbing another stile by a footpath sign.

Here bear right along a lane to a road junction. Cross over and bear slightly right on to Minchinhampton Common again, at a National Trust sign 'The Great Park'. Keep along the edge of the common, by a wall on the left, into Minchinhampton, turning left by the church to retrace your steps to the Market Square. ●

0	200	400	600	800 METRES	1	KILOMETRES
0	200	400	600 YARDS	¹⁄₂		MILES

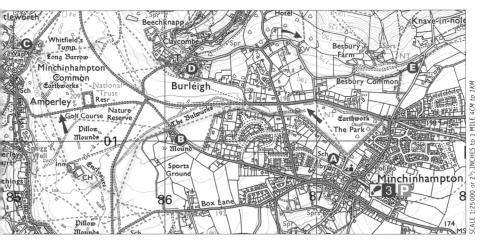

Northleach and Hampnett

Northleach and Hampnett

Start	Northleach
Distance	4 miles (6.5km)
Approximate time	2 hours
Parking	Northleach
Refreshments	Pubs, café and tearooms in Northleach
Ordnance Survey maps	Landranger 163 (Cheltenham & Cirencester) and Pathfinder 1090, SP 01/11 (Northleach & Andoversford)

*A very pleasant short walk in the valley of the infant River Leach,
mainly on field paths, most of which offer superb views over lovely
countryside. Two churches, both gems, form the main focal points:
one at Hampnett and the better-known one at Northleach itself.*

The 15th-century church at Northleach, with its magnificent south porch, is acclaimed as one of the grandest among the many 'wool churches' of the Cotswolds, its imposing Perpendicular tower dominating the streets of the small town. It reflects the heyday of the wool trade; inside are many monuments to the wool merchants who created the town's prosperity. Handsome stone and half-timbered buildings line the High Street and the inns are a reminder of Northleach's importance in the days of coach travel.

The church at Hampnett

From the Market Place walk north-westwards out of the town, passing the fire station on your left. At the traffic lights cross straight over the A429, keeping the Countryside Collection, an interesting museum of bygones housed in a former 18th-century prison, on the right. Cross a stile **A** opposite the abandoned Little Chef, follow the right-hand edge of a field to cross a ditch, and keep this on the left. Hampnett church can now be seen in the distance ahead. Walk round the field to reach its top right-hand corner by a wood romantically known as Prison Copse. Pass over a stile and continue, keeping by the wall on the right.

It can now be seen that Hampnett is a hilltop village, pretty both at a distance and close up. At the end of the wall bear right and climb up to the lane, turning left to reach the village.

The church, mainly Norman, looks charming from the outside, but its main impact comes from its painted interior. As the church notes say: '... whatever we may think of the result [of the restoration and decoration in the 19th

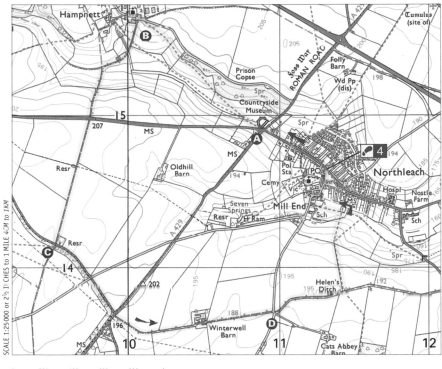

century] the courage and motives of the rector are worthy of admiration.' Although the result of this Victorian work remains controversial, there can be no denying that the richness of the decor emphasises the Norman features – the vaulting of the sanctuary is particularly notable.

Retrace a few steps back from the church and go down a track almost opposite the churchyard **B**. Pass through the farmyard at the bottom and then fork left where the track divides. Climb up the steep hill to the main road, admiring the fine view behind. Cross straight over the road and the pleasant green way continues on the other side.

Turn left where the track meets a road by a concealed reservoir **C**. Pass straight across the Yanworth road and across the A429 Stow to Cirencester trunk road, taking to a footpath reached through a small gate. This merges with another lovely green way by Winterwell Barn. After this building the lane becomes tarmacked.

Cross straight over the next road and take the rough track to the left **D**, not the tarmac road forking to the right. Northleach is still hidden by the crest of the hill, and remains so for some distance. Where the path suddenly dips, look for a gateway on the left with a yellow arrow symbol.

Turn left here towards the village, keeping to the left-hand side of the field. As you walk, Northleach slowly comes into view, with the church appearing last of all. Follow the path down through the grazing land and reach a playing-field by descending a steep bank. Head for the church to find a white-painted metal kissing-gate. Turn right into the lane by the school, turn right again and then left to return to the Market Place. ●

Blockley and Norcombe Wood

Start	Blockley
Distance	4½ miles (7.25km)
Approximate time	2½ hours
Parking	Roadside parking near church in Blockley
Refreshments	Pub at Blockley
Ordnance Survey maps	Landranger 151 (Stratford-upon-Avon) and Pathfinder 1043, SP 03/13 (Broadway & Chipping Campden)

This walk explores the pleasantly varied country lying to the west of Blockley, which nestles between wolds in the valley of Blockley Brook. After climbing gently across fields to reach the Moreton-in-Marsh to Broadway road and a fortunately brief stretch of walking along that busy road, you return across more fields and through some delightful woodland, with attractive views all the way.

By Cotswold standards Blockley is a large village; it is also delightfully unspoilt and uncommercialised, with a particularly interesting and varied history. In the Middle Ages it was owned by the bishops of Worcester and became a typical thriving woollen settlement. After the decline of the wool trade it turned to silk production, thereby prolonging its life as a textile centre. At its peak, in the early 19th century, there were eight mills in the village, mainly supplying silk to the ribbon manufacturers of Coventry. As a result of this enterprise, Blockley not only possesses the usual collection of dignified 17th- and 18th-century houses, but also has a number of unusually handsome 19th-century ones. Many of the former mills have now been converted to other uses, mostly as homes. Older than any of these is the fine medieval church, which retains its Norman chancel and contains monuments to the Northwick

family of nearby Northwick Park, successors to the bishops of Worcester as lords of the manor.

Starting by the church, walk through the village, passing to the right of the church, and bear to the right past the Crown Inn, continuing along to the bottom end of the village street. Ahead is a wooded valley which was landscaped by John Rushout, second Lord Northwick; it is called Dovedale, possibly after its better-known namesake in the Peak District. The route, however, turns right **Ⓐ**, at a public footpath sign, along a track which heads gently uphill through another narrow wooded valley called The Warren. Keep ahead at a fork, continuing uphill, at first through trees and later either across or along the right-hand edge of a series of fields, in a straight line. Pass a farm on the right, head across the middle of a field to a line of trees ahead and continue through them for a few yards to reach the Moreton-in-Marsh to Broadway road. **B**.

Turn right for just over ¼ mile (400m) and at a public bridleway stone **C**, turn right along a farm drive, passing through the narrow belt of trees that lines the road and continuing along the left-hand edge of a field. Shortly, where the wall on the left ends, turn left to follow the right-hand edge of a field, by a hedge on the right, to a farm track. Cross over and continue along the right-hand edge of the next field, by a wall on the right, to go through a gate and on to a road. Cross that and take the broad track in front, which heads downhill into woodland. At the point where the track curves right and starts to ascend **D** turn right off it along a tree-lined path to reach

the drive of Northwick Hill, which is the large house on the left. Keep ahead through the gate in front and turn right to head downhill across rough grass – there is no visible path – to a gate. Go through and follow a narrow but clear path through Norcombe Wood, a delightful ¾-mile (1.25km) woodland ramble. At first you descend the slope gently, bearing left on joining a lower path and continuing through the wood, finally dropping down to a gate at the far end.

Go through and head uphill across a field – there is no obvious path to follow – to a line of trees ahead and beyond these bear right to a wire fence on the edge of a playing field. Climb the fence and walk diagonally across the playing field, going through a gate in the far corner and along a track to a lane **E**. Turn right to follow the lane back into Blockley.

```
0    200   400   600   800 METRES  1
                                   KILOMETRES
                                   MILES
0    200   400   600 YARDS  ½
```

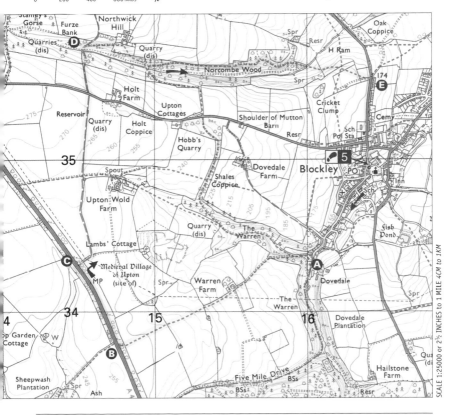

SCALE 1:25000 or 2½ INCHES to 1 MILE 4CM to 1KM

Burford, Fulbrook and Widford

Start	Burford
Distance	5½ miles (8.75km)
Approximate time	2½ hours
Parking	Burford
Refreshments	Pubs and cafés in Burford, two pubs in Fulbrook
Ordnance Survey maps	Landranger 163 (Cheltenham & Cirencester) and Pathfinder 1091, SP 21/31 (Burford & Witney (North))

There can be few more gentle walks than this, yet the scenery is rich and enjoyable. It is a walk of many meadows, with the last section along the banks of the River Windrush especially memorable. Burford is deservedly one of the Cotswolds' most famous beauty spots – well worth leaving plenty of time to explore.

A long, wide High Street lined with handsome stone buildings, sloping down to a medieval bridge over the River Windrush, makes Burford one of the most appealing of Cotswold towns. It has a large number of distinguished houses dating from the 14th to the 18th century, many of them formerly belonging to wool merchants, and a magnificent 'wool church'.

Start the walk by the bridge at the bottom of High Street. Cross the bridge and turn right on to the Chipping Norton road, which in a short distance takes you into the village of Fulbrook. Pass Meadow End on the right and shortly afterwards look out carefully for a concealed yellow-waymarked stile on the right **A**. Climb it, and another one a few yards ahead and turn left past the backs of gardens, climbing two more stiles. Go through a kissing-gate on the right and continue along a path between wooden fences to another stile. Climb that, walk along the left-

hand edge of a field and turn left at the end of it over a stile and along a path, bearing left on to a lane which has a mixture of new houses and old cottages. This lovely byway leads back to the main road in the centre of Fulbrook, where the interesting Norman church is worth a visit.

Turn right along the road and, after passing an ancient milestone in the wall on the right and at the bottom of a dip in the road, find a footpath sign and a path branching off on the right. At first keep to the right-hand edge of a field, but where the field edge curves slightly to the right walk in a straight line across the large sloping field – there is no obvious path – heading gently uphill to the far corner. Here go through a gap in a wall and diagonally across the next field; pass through another gap and keep on, still in a straight line, towards the trees ahead.

Turn right on to a track **B** which enters the wood, Widley Copse, and on

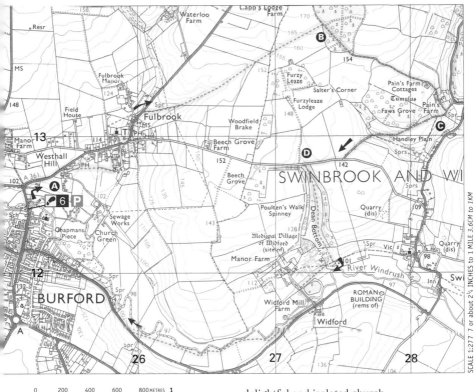

SCALE 1:277 7 or about 2¼ INCHES to 1 MILE 3.6CM to 1KM

```
0    200   400   600   800 METRES  1
                                      KILOMETRES
                                      MILES
0    200   400   600 YARDS   ½
```

emerging from it keep ahead along the farm track which descends to Pain's Farm. After passing the farm continue down the hill for about 50 yds (46m) before turning right and walking up a stony track **C**. Go through a metal gate at the top to walk through a meadow with a wood on the right. The track descends gently, leaving the trees, to reach a gate at the bottom of the field. It continues by climbing up the next field to reach a lane.

Turn right and follow the lane down to some trees. At the bottom of a dip turn left over a stile **D** and into a lovely broad and verdant valley, the route waymarked to Widford and Swinbrook. This part of the walk is over too soon: after just ½ mile (800m) you climb a stile and head towards a farm. At a finger-post turn right to go through a gateway and on past Widford church on the right. This small,

delightful and isolated church – isolated because the former village of Widford was abandoned, presumably at the time of the Black Death – dates mainly from the 13th century. It was built on the site of an ancient Roman villa and some of the villa's ornate mosaic flooring still survives. The church also contains some rare medieval wall paintings in the nave and chancel.

Continue to a lane, at which point you turn left, turning right along a road after crossing over the millstream. After 200 yds (184m) fork right on to a footpath which follows the southern bank of the River Windrush. Now there is a delightful riverside walk: the river meanders unhurriedly and for the most part the path follows its course faithfully over a succession of stiles. After the fourth stile follow a line of waymarked trees away from the river up to another stile and then on to a road. Turn right and follow the road into Burford. ●

Bibury and the River Coln

Start	Bibury
Distance	6 miles (9.5km)
Approximate time	3 hours
Parking	Roadside parking by river at Bibury or car park in front of Arlington Mill Museum
Refreshments	Pubs and cafés at Bibury and Arlington, pub at Coln St Aldwyn
Ordnance Survey maps	Landranger 163 (Cheltenham & Cirencester) and Pathfinder 1114, SP 00/10 (Cirencester)

This relaxing walk takes you through the gentle and pleasant scenery of the Coln valley on the south-eastern fringes of the Cotswolds. Fine views extend for miles over wide and undulating country towards the upper Thames valley and beyond to the line of the Berkshire Downs. There are some delightful riverside meadows and woodlands, and two enchanting Cotswold villages.

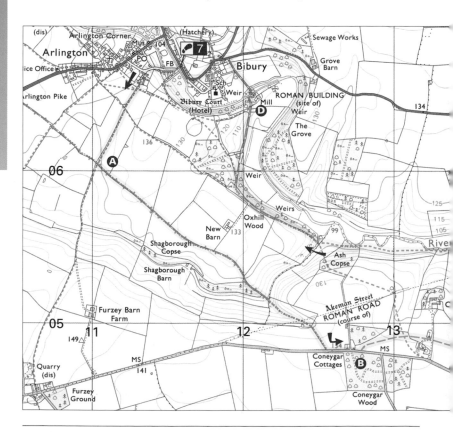

The eminent Victorian and Cotswold inhabitant William Morris considered Bibury the most beautiful village in England. Its attractions are manifest: the peaceful Coln flowing between Bibury and Arlington, although the two villages are to all intents and purposes one, picturesque 17th- and 18th-century cottages, charming little squares and greens, the 17th-century corn mill at Arlington – now a working museum – and the splendid church, once the property of Osney Abbey near Oxford. This fine building includes work dating from every century from the 12th to the 15th and still retains some vestiges of the Saxon church, as well as two fine Norman doorways. The 15th-century west tower is unusual in that it rises above the north aisle,

giving the church a curiously asymmetrical appearance.

The walk begins by the clapper bridge over the River Coln. Cross it and walk past Rack Isle and then the picturesque Arlington Row, both owned by the National Trust. The former is a water-meadow, given its name because it was where cloth was dried on wooden racks after the fulling process. The latter is a row of 17th-century cottages, built for cloth weavers and one of the most photographed collections of cottages in England. Continue uphill to a small green and at a public footpath sign to Ready Token turn left along a track between houses to a metal gate. Go through and keep ahead to the next gate by a complex footpath sign. Pass through that gate and continue along a series of field edges, with wall and hedges variously on the right, to a metal gate.

Do not go through but turn left **Ⓐ** in front of it along a broad path which you keep along for 1¼ miles (2km): first along the right-hand and then along the left-hand edge of fields, later dropping down to skirt a copse on the right, going through a metal gate and continuing uphill to pass through another gate, finally following a stony track to reach a road. The path is pleasant, wide and easy to follow, giving attractive views across gently rolling country.

At the road turn left for 300 yds (276m) and just after passing two houses on the left turn left **Ⓑ**, at a bridleway sign, through a gate and then turn right to head across the middle of a field – there is no visible path – to a metal gate at the far end. Go through it and continue ahead, passing in front of a house and across a farm drive, to go through another metal gate. Now keep along a narrow but clear path across the middle of a field,

SCALE 1:25000 or 2½ INCHES to 1 MILE 4CM to 1KM

passing through another metal gate and continuing along the field edge, by a wall on the right. After the wall ends keep ahead along a grassy path which heads down through a beautiful group of large, widely spaced beeches to a gate. Pass through that and bear left downhill to a gate where you join the River Coln **C**.

Go through on to the road and turn left over the bridge if you want to explore the attractive village of Coln St Aldwyn which has a fine old church, delightful pub and imposing Tudor manor house.

Otherwise turn left in front of the gate and walk across riverside meadows, below the wooded bank of The Sidelands on the left, to pass through a gate into the woods, continuing along a wide path. Keep ahead on leaving the woods, between fields on the right and the edge of the woods on the left and past the end of the woods continue along the field edge, by a hedge on the left, later rejoining the river. Now there is a lovely stretch of riverside walking by

the placid waters of the River Coln across peaceful meadows fringed with trees. The route continues through two gates, skirts Ash Copse on the left, carries on through another gate at the far end and then bears slightly left across the meadow towards Oxhill Wood ahead. Climb over a stone stile, or go through a gate to the left of it, to enter the wood.

Follow a clear path which heads up to a gate. Go through and continue along the edge of the wood on the right to pass through two more gates before bearing slightly right through another gate and dropping down, finally leaving the wood. In front is a most attractive view looking towards Bibury with the river to the right, woodland clothing its opposite bank. Continue through two more gates and after the second one, by a footpath sign, walk along a tarmac drive which bears first right, then left **D**, passes a former mill and then crosses the river. Continue – with a fine view of the 17th-century Bibury Court Hotel, formerly the manor house, on the left – up to a road and turn left through the village back to the starting point. ●

The picturesque Arlington Row at Bibury

Blenheim Park

Start	Woodstock
Distance	6½ miles (10.5km)
Approximate time	3½ hours
Parking	Woodstock
Refreshments	Pubs and cafés at Woodstock, pubs at Old Woodstock
Ordnance Survey maps	Landranger 164 (Oxford) and Pathfinder 1092, SP 41/51 (Woodstock)

Most of this walk is within the boundaries of Blenheim Park, one of the most superb examples of landscaped parkland in the country. The scenic highlight is towards the end – magnificent views across the lake to the great palace, built for John Churchill, first Duke of Marlborough, and named after his greatest military triumph.

Woodstock, a handsome and bustling little town with many dignified 17th- and 18th-century houses lining its busy streets, is particularly well-endowed with shops, cafés, inns and restaurants to cater for visitors, many of them *en route* to Blenheim Palace. From Saxon times this area was a royal manor and the town grew up at the entrance to the park that was first enclosed in the early 12th century.

Start at the corner of High Street and Oxford Street and head northwards along Oxford Street out of the town. The Victory Column, a prominent landmark ahead, is in sight for much of the time. Cross over the River Glyme to enter Old Woodstock, which was the site of the original settlement until the 'new town' was founded in the 12th century by Henry II, and by a telephone box and bus shelter turn right **A** and pass through some railings into Westland Way. After 50 yds (46m) turn left into Rosamund Drive and continue through a new housing estate until you reach a metal gate and a public footpath sign where the road ends. Bear left and shortly afterwards right to keep along the left-hand edge of a field, by the backs of some houses and gardens. After passing the end of the houses on the left the path veers half-right and heads diagonally across a field, bearing left on reaching a hedge and then continuing through a gap in the hedge and straight across the middle of the next field. Pass to the right of farm buildings and continue, heading gently downhill to go through a narrow gap in a hedge at the bottom end of the field and on to a lane **B**.

Blenheim Palace and gardens

Turn left for ¹/₂ mile (800m) up to the A34, cross over and continue in the direction of an Oxfordshire Way sign between an avenue of trees to a door in the boundary wall of Blenheim Park. Go through it into the park, immediately climb a stile and bear right to join a track. The definitive route heads straight across the field to the farm ahead but there is no stile in the wire fence in front and no obvious path. A waymarked alternative is to walk along the track as far as a fork where you bear left to climb a stile and turn left, heading for the farm.

Keep to the right of the farm and continue along a broad, straight track which follows the line of Akeman Street, a Roman road that linked Cirencester and St Albans. Go through

a gate and keep ahead, crossing a straight drive and on through another gate to continue across the flat, landscaped parkland. Soon you pass The Clump, a prominent, isolated circle of trees on the left. Continue to a line of trees ahead, enter them and just before meeting the park wall again turn left **C** along a track, which runs parallel to the wall, for 200 yds (184m). Look out for a footbridge on the left, cross it and continue to a yellow-waymarked post at the edge of a field.

Head across the field in a straight line, bearing slightly right to keep by a low, grassy bank on the right, to reach a track. Turn left along it to a junction where you turn right to go through a gate. Immediately climb a fence on the left and turn right across the grass – there is no path but keep to the left of the nearest group of trees in front – to reach a wire fence by a stile and footpath sign. Climb the stile and turn right by the wire fence on the right, skirting the clump of trees in front and continuing over a stile to the left of a farm ⑩. Now walk for just over ¼ mile (400m) along a broad tarmac drive, following it as it bends to the left and continues to a junction. Here turn sharp right along a drive which curves left downhill, continues over a cattle-grid and starts to ascend.

At this point ⑭ turn left and walk across the grass, below a wooded bank on the right, towards the end of the lake. Climb a stile in the wooden fence on the left and keep ahead to pick up a definite track which winds along the left side of a narrow arm of the lake. On broadening out at the main part of the lake, the track turns sharply to the left and continues above the lake, passing some magnificent old beeches. Now follows the high point of the walk. For the next ¼ mile (400m) the constantly changing views across the lake to the vast bulk of Blenheim Palace and the impressive Grand Bridge are breathtaking. Here you can truly appreciate the effect produced by the combined efforts of two different geniuses: Sir John Vanbrugh who designed the palace and 'Capability' Brown who landscaped the park.

Blenheim Park was originally a royal park carved from neighbouring Wychwood Forest by Henry I in the 12th century. The same monarch also built a hunting lodge, subsequently enlarged into a palace and used by almost all medieval and Tudor kings. During the 17th-century Civil Wars between Charles I and Parliament it suffered damage and subsequently fell into ruin. A major transformation came in 1704 when in recognition of his victory over the French at Blenheim the royal manor of Woodstock was given to John Churchill, created first Duke of

Marlborough by a grateful Queen Anne. The remains of the old palace were cleared to be replaced by Sir John Vanbrugh's massive Italian-style mansion, one of the grandest palaces in England, with a magnificent series of state rooms full of superb tapestries, paintings, sculpture and furniture. Winston Churchill was born here in 1874, an event commemorated by a Churchill exhibition. Surrounding the palace are the formal gardens and beyond them the informal 2500-acre (1012 ha) park, landscaped in the contemporary fashion by 'Capability' Brown about 50 years after the palace was completed.

The track keeps above the lake, bearing right to meet a tarmac drive near the end of the Grand Bridge. Turn left along the drive for ¼ mile (400m) to where it dips slightly. Here turn right ⑭ across open grassland, keeping for a while by a wire fence on the left and passing to the right of the Victory Column, erected in commemoration of the Duke of Marlborough's victories over the French. From here there is a magnificent view to the right of the north front of the palace.

Continue past the column, bearing slightly right downhill to a tarmac drive by a house and the corner of the lake. Cross the drive, continue in front of the house and turn right along the drive ahead past the end of the lake. Soon bear left off the drive ⑭ along an uphill path, from which there is a final glorious view across the lake to the façade of the palace, heading across the grass towards houses at the point where the path curves to the left. Here go through a wooden kissing-gate in the park wall, continue ahead between houses to the main road in Old Woodstock and turn right to retrace your steps over the River Glyme and up the hill to Woodstock town centre. ●

Brimpsfield and Syde

Start	Layby at Gloucester Beeches off the A417 just to the south of the turning to Brimpsfield
Distance	6½ miles (10.5km)
Approximate time	3½ hours
Parking	Layby at Gloucester Beeches
Refreshments	None
Ordnance Survey maps	Landranger 163 (Cheltenham & Cirencester) and Pathfinder 1089, SO 81/91 (Gloucester & Birdlip)

More than half of this walk is through woodland, much of it highly attractive. Apart from the detour to see Syde church, there are few gradients to fear. Mud is likely to be more of a problem, for much of the route is along bridleways popular with horse-riders.

Begin near the northern end of the long layby where there are public footpath and bridleway signs. Turn along a track, after a few yards climb a stile just to the right of a metal gate and walk along the left edge of a field, by a wall on the left. Go through a metal gate, continue along the left edge of the next field and after the next gate bear right to follow a track gently downhill, passing a waymarked post, curving right to keep alongside the right edge of woodland. Just before reaching a blue-waymarked gate, turn sharp left **A** along a track that leads into the wood. At the end of the conifers bear left, following a waymark and keeping to the bottom of the valley with a ditch to the right. This is soon crossed by a bridge leading into a pleasant meadow – continue along the edge of woods.

At the end of the woods, in another long meadow, fork left at a footpath junction going up the shoulder of the hill keeping the small copse at the top on the left. Pass through the gate ahead at the end of the farm buildings. Turn left on to the lane and then right on to

the road to reach Syde church **B**, with its small saddleback tower. The 12th-century church is a place of great character and peace, still retaining gas lighting and box pews.

Retrace your steps to the footpath, passing through the gate to the right of the barn. This barn dates from the 14th century and was the district's great tithe barn.

Head down towards the cottages of Caudle Green on the other side of the valley. Go through the yellow-waymarked gate at the bottom and walk past a cottage to the lane. Turn left and at the base of the hill take the steep path on the right to cut a corner. Climb through the village, passing Tudor Cottage on the right, to find a gateway on the left with a blue waymark **C**.

Follow the right-hand edge of the field,

eventually dropping to the wood below. Turn right through conifers (do not go through the gap in the wall below). The path descends to the bottom of a valley where it meets a sandy track – a pond is on the left. Follow this track through trees for the next 2 miles (3.25km) or so. When you come to a gate go through and climb briefly up the side of the valley, then drop back to the bottom, still following the blue waymark. Horses have made some sections muddy, but it is passable with care and good boots. A pond is passed on the left before you meet the road at Climperwell Cottage. Cross the road to the woods just to the left of the cottage drive and keep the wall on the right through the meadow. Before the gateway leading into another tree-fringed meadow, turn right **D** up a slope to a stile with a yellow waymark. A gloomy section opens into a field, and the path follows its edge with the wood on the left. It enters the

wood again to climb up to reach more fields at the top. Keep the hedge on the left to reach the road.

Cross this – the waymark is now blue again – and follow the edges of three fields directly towards Brimpsfield. In the last field the bridleway becomes a footpath again. Walk down the short lane into the centre of the village.

Turn left down the drive to Brimpsfield Park and a lovely view soon opens up on the left, with the 15th-century tower of Brimpsfield church prominent. As you proceed, the traffic on Ermin Street, the A417, is both audible and visible on the crest of the valley. Pass through the farmyard (note the lintel of the barn with its collection of horseshoes) and through the gateway of the house, keeping the house to the left by walking down the track to pass two small lakes. Dogs should be on leads here.

After passing through a blue waymarked gate, keep ahead **A** along an ascending track to retrace your steps to the start.   ●

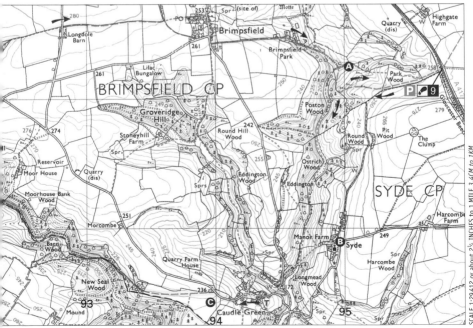

SCALE 1:29412 or about 2¼ INCHES to 1 MILE 3.4CM to 1KM

Broadway and Broadway Tower

Start	Broadway
Distance	4 miles (6.5km)
Approximate time	2 hours
Parking	Broadway
Refreshments	Pubs, cafés and restaurants at Broadway, café at Broadway Tower Country Park
Ordnance Survey maps	Landranger 150 (Worcester & The Malverns) and Pathfinder 1043, SP 03/13 (Broadway & Chipping Campden)

This walk follows a simple 'across, up, across and down' pattern, with the easy downhill stretch fortuitously coming at the end. Starting in the centre of Broadway at the foot of the Cotswold escarpment, the walk first heads across fields to Broadway Old Church, then climbs through woodland to reach the top of the scarp. It continues along the edge to Broadway Tower, considered one of the finest viewpoints in England, before descending back into the village. On the latter part of the walk a magnificent vista across the Vale of Evesham stretches out in front of you.

Broadway nestles below the escarpment at the foot of steep Fish Hill on the edge of the Vale of Evesham. It is another of the showplace villages of the Cotswolds – as its teeming crowds and traffic readily testify – despite lacking the normal attractions of a river, an outstanding building or any well-known amenities. Its popularity lies in its situation and the overall charm of its buildings, mostly handsome 17th- and 18th-century houses. A wide, dignified and long High Street, the Broad Way, slopes down and broadens out to a triangular green around which are grouped houses and cottages, inns and tea-rooms, gift and antique shops. It was its position as a staging post on the main coach route between London and Worcester that brought prosperity to Broadway in the 18th century; later it became a fashionable place for writers and artists, starting with William Morris, one of the Pre-Raphaelite fraternity and a highly influential artist, craftsman and critic of Victorian industrialism.

The starting point is at the bottom of the long High Street by the war memorial. Walk up the street and opposite the Horse and Hound Inn turn right **Ⓐ**, at a signpost to 'Recreation Ground and Old Church', along a path between high walls on the left and a hedge on the right. This soon continues through an attractive avenue of trees and along the edge of a recreation ground, by a metal fence on the right.

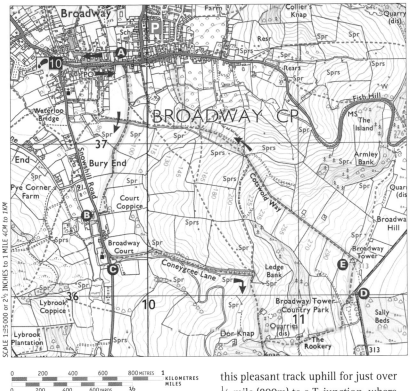

0   200   400   600   800 METRES   1
                                        KILOMETRES
                                        MILES
0   200   400   600 YARDS   ½

To the right the tower of the 19th-century New Church stands out prominently. Climb a stile, continue along clear grassy paths over a succession of stiles and across several fields, following yellow waymarks all the time. In the last field follow the field boundary round to the right to go through a gate and on to a road **B**.

Turn left along the road for about 300 yds (276m), passing the impressive buildings of Broadway Court on the right and beyond that the delightful and attractive Old Church dedicated to St Eadburgha, ³⁄₄ mile (1.25km) south of the village. It is an imposing cruciform building with a fine 14th-century tower and the interior is a fascinating and harmonious blend of Norman and Gothic features. Opposite the church turn left **C** through ornamental gates, at a public footpath sign to Broadway Tower, along a wide tree-lined track, passing to the left of a lodge. Follow this pleasant track uphill for just over ¹⁄₂ mile (800m) to a T-junction, where you turn right. Go through a gate about 50 yds (46m) ahead and bear to the left, still walking uphill, across a field towards a bungalow. Bear right in front of the bungalow, pass through a gate and keep ahead to a metal gate at the edge of woodland. Do not go through that gate but turn left through another one along another uphill track, later joining a lane and continuing to the top of the escarpment.

Just before reaching Broadway Country Park car park turn left **D** over a stile to walk along the edge of the scarp. A ladder-stile on the right leads to a café; the walk keeps ahead through a gate and along a grassy path, by a fence on the right, to Broadway Tower which at a height of 1024ft (312m) is the second highest point in the Cotswolds. The views from here over the Vale of Evesham, Broadway, Bredon Hill and the distant Malverns are magnificent, and in exceptionally clear conditions the Shropshire Hills and

Black Mountains can also be seen. The tower is a folly, built in 1798 by James Wyatt for the Earl of Coventry, as a present for his wife, and is undoubtedly one of the most impressive viewpoints to be found in the whole of England. Since 1972 it has been the focal point of a small country park and houses exhibitions about the tower itself, William Morris and the Cotswold woollen industry.

Now follows the easy descent to Broadway village along part of the Cotswold Way. Turn left past the tower **E** down to a stile in the corner of a field, climb over and continue downhill, across a succession of fields, through several gates and over a number of stiles, following yellow-waymarked signs all the way and with outstanding views over the Vale of Evesham and beyond in front all the while. After crossing an area of rough pasture go through a gap in a hedge where the yellow waymarks indicate that the path divides. Here bear right, heading diagonally across the field to climb a stile in the bottom corner. Continue across a brook, over two more stiles and on to the road where you turn left down Broadway High Street to return to the starting point. ●

Poppy field near Broadway

The Guitings and Guiting Wood

Start	Car park at the western end of Critchford Lane, about ¾ mile (1.25km) south-west of Kineton
Distance	6½ miles (10.5km)
Approximate time	3 hours
Parking	After passing into the gated section of the road to the west of Critchford Ford, turn left at the crossroads to find a small gated car park half-hidden amongst chestnut trees and sheep-pens
Refreshments	Pubs at Kineton and Guiting Power
Ordnance Survey maps	Landranger 163 (Cheltenham & Cirencester) and Pathfinder 1067, SP 02/12 (Stow-on-the-Wold)

This is a walk well worth doing, both for the section through Guiting Wood, a large expanse of woodland mainly covering the slopes of the valley of the little Castlett stream, and the enjoyable interludes along quiet lanes and through fields. In addition, three small attractive villages are passed through.

Turn to the right from the car park and head back to Critchford Lane; turn left along the lane so that the lovely manor house is on the right. Excavations in the meadow here have uncovered the remains of an Iron Age farmstead dating from the 3rd to 1st centuries BC. The site has produced valuable finds, including a wide variety of pottery. It seems that animals were herded here, and grain harvested, the latter being stored in a series of pits.

After the field gate at the end of this meadow turn right to pass behind the manor house. Before the next gate turn to the left off the made-up drive and follow the line of a wooden fence. This leads up to the edge of Guiting Wood.

Keep the wood on the right for the length of two long fields and just before the end of the second of these look for a clearly waymarked path into

the woods Ⓐ. You will pass by an ancient right-of-way stone on the left. Timber operations make the following short stretch very muddy in wet weather and brambles add to the difficulties. In autumn, however, the

---

In Guiting Wood

colours of the wide variety of trees are an adequate compensation.

At a footpath crossroads keep straight on; the way now starts to descend, and soon becomes steeper. The trees here are young and scrubby, and the path slippery. Turn right at the footpath junction at the bottom. The path now is very narrow and overgrown in places and ends where a stile gives on to a lane **B**. Turn right here for an easier passage through the remainder of Guiting Wood.

The lane leads mainly downhill until it crosses a tiny stream, with a pumping station on the left. Hazel trees abound here. Past the stream the lane climbs quite steeply; keep along it, ignoring various inviting alternatives. The view back from the summit of the hill at Louisehill Plantation towards Guiting Wood illustrates the wide variety of trees it contains.

Now the lane descends gently to Temple Guiting where it meets a busier road which we follow by turning right to Kineton. At this point a detour can be made to visit the church at Temple Guiting **C**, which is reached in three minutes by turning left at the junction to find almost immediately a footpath on the right leading to it. The small village lies ahead on the other side of the River Windrush.

The church dates from the 12th century, the heyday of the Knights Templar who gave the village its name. The most notable features of this lovely, tranquil building for visitors to see are the remains of medieval glass in the middle window on the south side (the Metropolitan Museum in New York is said to own the other figures which came from this set) and the remarkably ornate arms of George II worked in plaster by John Switzer in 1742 which are mounted above the entry to the bell-tower.

Returning to the junction by New Barn Farm, turn away from the church to follow the lane to Kineton, with lovely views of hills and woodland to the east. Here the Half Way House is noted for its food and drink.

Continue along the lane and after ½ mile (800m) look for a waymarked footpath on the right **D**, opposite a pair of semi-detached cottages. This

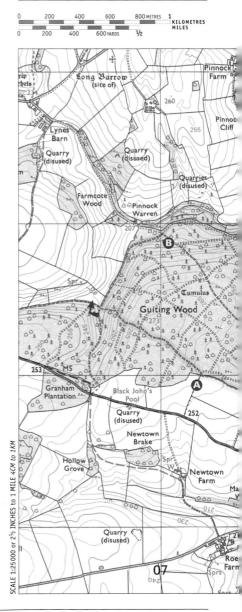

leads across a field to follow a hedge on the left. A lane is crossed and the footpath continues on the other side. Cross a stream by a footbridge and then keep the stream on the left, finally crossing a stile to reach a lane which leads to the village green of Guiting Power. There are two pubs to be found in this village: the Farmers' Arms downhill from the war memorial, about 200 yds (184m) away, and Ye Olde Inne (or Th' Ollow Bottom) which is passed on the way out of the village by turning to the right at the war memorial. The village church, though heavily restored by the Victorians, still retains two Norman doorways.

Just after the village sign, walking north-westwards out of the village, turn to the right down a lane marked with an 'Unsuitable for Motors' sign. Leave the lane by the sandy track on the left, which follows the contours of the hill for a pleasant ten minutes of walking until the starting point comes into view on the right. ●

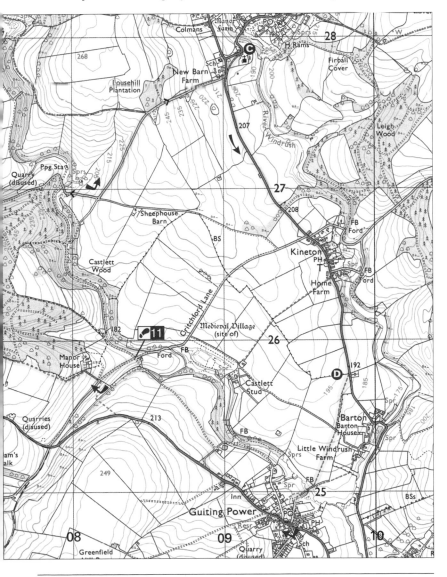

Sapperton and Daneway

Start	Sapperton
Distance	4½ miles (7.25km)
Approximate time	3 hours
Parking	By Sapperton church
Refreshments	Pub at Daneway Bridge
Ordnance Survey maps	Landranger 163 (Cheltenham & Cirencester) and Pathfinder 1113, SO 80/90 (Stroud)

Despite a lack of open views, this is a walk of great variety and historic interest. The final part of the walk follows the course of the abandoned Thames and Severn Canal and passes the portal of Kinnerton Tunnel, a memorable monument to a bygone era.

Sapperton church is dedicated to St Kenelm, whose shrine was at Winchcombe Abbey. There was a church here in Norman times but very little of its fabric survives in the present structure, most of which dates from the early 18th century. Much of the magnificent woodwork came from the old manor house which stood close by on the north side of the church overlooking the valley.

The walk starts from the telephone-box on the lane opposite the church, at a blue-waymarked bridleway. Note the diversion in the first field which entails crossing the stile on the right and then following the field edge with the hedge on the left.

Go through the gate at The Leasowes and into a belt of trees, still following the blue waymark to another gate leading into a lovely long meadow. At the top right-hand corner of this **Ⓐ** turn left on to a track to descend to a footpath junction at a gateway – the fine house which is in view up ahead is Pinbury Park. Turn to the left just before the gateway, continuing downhill and now following a yellow

waymark. Bear to the right in the woods where the path divides. The trees seen here are mainly beech. Soon the bottom of the Frome valley is reached (note the blue waymark on a beech tree here where two streams unite). Go through a gate and turn right up a sunken track where the constant passage of hoofed traffic has made the going rather muddy. Once you pass an arched elm you are nearly at the top. Keep straight on when tracks cross to reach a farm track at the summit **Ⓑ**. This is a pleasant open walk across a very long field.

Evening at Sapperton

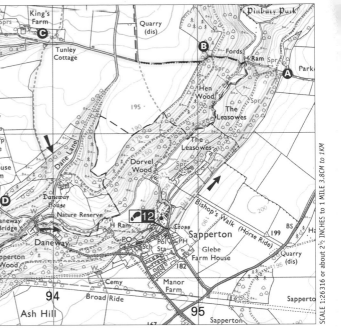

SCALE 1:26316 or about 2½ INCHES to 1 MILE 3.8CM to 1KM

Cross straight over the road and head for Tunley Cottage on a tarmac lane. Immediately before the cottage **C** turn left up the bank by steps which take the footpath behind the building. Make for the hedge ahead and then keep it to the right; the fields here are vast and the going can be uncomfortable if they have been recently cultivated.

Head for the gate in the right-hand corner of the last of the very large fields – a big house, Daneway, is straight ahead. Go through the gate and continue straight ahead to the bottom of the valley. Do not cross over the road but after passing two stiles close together turn right and then climb a third one into a meadow with a scattering of hawthorn trees. Keep the fence to the right and follow a vague track towards woods. Cross the road **D** to enter them – this is the Siccaridge Wood Nature Reserve. The path here is a delight to walk: the undergrowth has been cleared back and wild flowers and butterflies abound.

As the path begins to descend the trees close in. At a clearing there is a footpath crossways; here bear half-left – effectively this means going straight on – and the path begins to descend steeply. Where it divides again bear left to go down to a bridge **E**. Cross it and turn left to follow the right bank of the Thames and Severn Canal. Opened in 1789 and finally abandoned in 1927, this canal was built to link the Thames with the Stroudwater Canal, thus creating a continuous waterway between the Thames and the Severn. The path follows the old tow-path and every so often the ruined masonry of locks can be seen: in some cases the drop looks perilous. A wooden footbridge takes the path to the left bank of the canal, and Daneway Bridge soon appears ahead.

Cross the bridge and take the footpath on the left to Sapperton. The entrance to the canal tunnel (2½ miles/ 4km long) is made even more sinister by the ruins of the house which stand by it. Cross the top of the portal of the tunnel to follow the footpath back over meadows to Sapperton church. ●

Dyrham Park and West Littleton

Start	Car park and picnic area off the A46 just south of the Tormarton Interchange with the M4 (Junction 18)
Distance	5½ miles (8.75km)
Approximate time	3 hours
Parking	Car park to the south of Tormarton Interchange
Refreshments	Sometimes a mobile kiosk at the car park
Ordnance Survey maps	Landranger 172 (Bristol & Bath) and Pathfinder 1167, ST 67/77 (Bristol (East))

This is a delightful walk with wonderful views to the north-west from this southernmost outlier of the Cotswolds. There is a fair amount of field walking involved – be prepared for some hard muddy going – and the walk includes a stretch along the edge of the attractive Dyrham Deer Park.

From the car park a tarmac path leads to the main road. Turn right and at the end of the layby cross it to a footpath opposite. This is almost a lost way, the undergrowth between the hedges on either side having almost engulfed the footpath, but it is walkable.

At the end of the enclosed section **Ⓐ** you may have difficulty as there is no easy headland to walk on. It is best to pass through an overgrown gate entrance on the right and then, keeping the hedge on the left, head south to the lane which runs parallel to the M4. Having reached the lane at a point close to where the electricity lines cross it, turn left for about 200 yds (184m) and then right on to a bridleway to West Littleton, Hinton and Dyrham. This is a pleasant farm track called Wallsend Lane which winds its way uphill.

The village of West Littleton appears ahead, the unusual belfry of its church standing out on its right-hand side like the turret of a baronial castle. Turn left at the lane to reach the village, then right at the telephone-box to follow the

path into the churchyard **Ⓑ**. According to notes in the church, the building was largely rebuilt by T.H. White in 1855, but the 13th-century canopied bellcote, of which there are very few remaining examples in the Cotswolds, survived.

Leave the churchyard by a stone stile in the west wall and go through a gate by a riding school to enter a paddock. Cross this to the gate opposite and cross a narrow meadow to a ladder-stile over a stone wall. Then follow the hedge down to a farm track.

The right of way now lies directly across three cultivated fields. Cross the farm track and head across the field, making for a large stone set in the hedge on the far side. You will also be making for the left end of the planting of trees on the skyline. After the large flat stone, which serves as a stile, continue in the same direction to reach the next hedgerow. The footpath passes through a small gap in this and then heads across the next field towards the main road where there is a footpath signpost. Cross the road to the stone

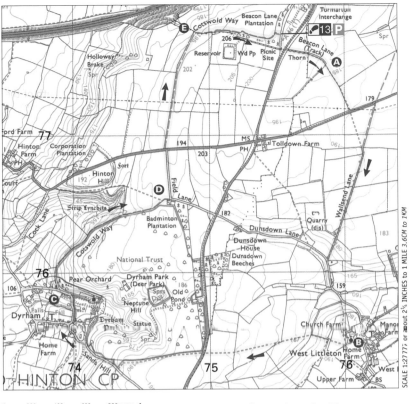

Scale note (right margin): SCALE 1:27777 or about 2¼ INCHES to 1 MILE 3.6CM to 1KM

Scale bar:
```
0   200   400   600   800 METRES  1
                                    KILOMETRES
                                    MILES
0   200   400   600 YARDS   ½
```

steps opposite and then continue by the wire fence on the edge of the deer park. Turn right at the road downhill into Dyrham village and then turn right towards the church, at a Cotswold Way sign, along a shady lane. To the right you will soon see Dyrham House and church through some ornamental gates.

Dyrham House, a splendid mansion set amidst gardens and an extensive deer park, is well worth a visit. It was built by William Talman towards the end of the 17th century. The attractive church at Dyrham dates mostly from the 15th century but retains a Norman arcade in the nave.

Shortly after a left bend you turn right on to a bridleway, signposted to Hinton Hill, West Littleton and Tormarton, which is part of the Cotswold Way **C**. Go through the trees to the gate to gain access to Hinton Hill,

a magnificent viewpoint. The strange grooves on the hill ahead are strip lynchets, or cultivation terraces, probably medieval. Above these is a hill fort. Walk along the edges of two fields, following a wall on the right along the shoulder of the hill, and pass through the gate at the top. There is another viewpoint here, with Bristol clearly visible. Continue to a lane **D** and turn left by a Cotswold Way sign. Cross straight over a more important lane to continue to follow the bridleway, keeping the hedge on the left, down a long field. From this point the M4 motorway can clearly be seen winding its way through the valley below.

Turn to the right after crossing the ditch at the bottom of the field **E**, following the edge of a belt of trees. The path then gradually bends to the left around the wood, and at the end of this bend look for a waymark on the right pointing through the trees. The path soon returns to the starting point. ●

Chipping Campden and Dover's Hill

Start	Chipping Campden
Distance	5 miles (8km)
Approximate time	2½ hours
Parking	Main street at Chipping Campden
Refreshments	Pubs and cafés at Chipping Campden
Ordnance Survey maps	Landrangers 150 (Worcester & The Malverns) and 151 (Stratford-upon-Avon) and Pathfinder 1043, SP 03/13 (Broadway & Chipping Campden)

From Chipping Campden the route proceeds uphill, along the first section of the Cotswold Way, on to the Cotswold escarpment at the magnificent vantage point of Dover's Hill overlooking the Vale of Evesham. Then it descends, with splendid views in front, before regaining the escarpment via a steep woodland track, finally dropping back into Chipping Campden. The walk leaves plenty of time to explore one of the finest of Cotswold towns, but despite its modest length there are two fairly energetic climbs.

With its many mellowed stone houses, 17th-century Market Hall and 15th-century church, Chipping Campden is the Cotswold wool town *par excellence*. Its curving High Street is acclaimed as one of the finest in the country, with buildings of all ages from the 14th century onwards – but mostly a reflection of the town's prosperity in the 'golden age' of the Cotswold wool trade, in the later Middle Ages and on into the 16th and 17th centuries. The church at Chipping Campden is a fine example of a wool church, its Perpendicular tower dominating the town around it.

Start at the Market Hall by walking along the High Street away from the church and turn right **A**, at a Cotswold Way sign, along a lane signposted 'Back Ends and Hoo Lane'. Where the lane bends right keep ahead past a thatched cottage on the left, and continue on past a bridleway sign to Dover's Hill and Aston Subedge, after which the lane becomes a rough uphill track. Climb a stile, continue steeply uphill to climb another stile and keep ahead a few yards until you reach a road.

Turn left for about 50 yds (46m) and at a public footpath and Cotswold Way sign turn right **B** along the edge of a field, by a hedge on the right. Climb a stile, turn left and walk across to the triangulation pillar on the summit of Dover's Hill **C**. From a few yards ahead on the edge of the scarp there is an outstanding view over the Vale of Evesham. Dover's Hill is named after a local lawyer, Robert Dover, who in 1612 founded some famous games here, nicknamed the Cotswold 'Olympicks'. They were very popular but eventually

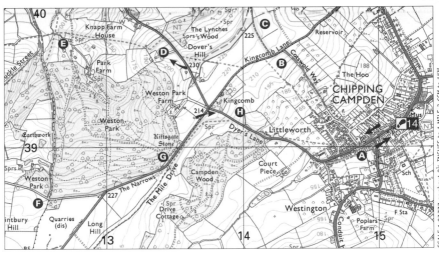

SCALE 1:27777 or about 2¼ INCHES to 1 MILE 3.6CM to 1KM

violence and drunkenness led to their abolition in 1853, though they were revived in 1951 and are still held, albeit somewhat more sedately.

Continue along the top of the scarp and bear right by a toposcope to head downhill, making for a gate on the left, and continue on to a lane. Turn right down the lane, turn left over a stile **D** at the first footpath sign on the left, and walk along the top edge of a field, by a hedge and fence on the left. Look out for a footpath sign on the left, turn half-right and follow the direction of the sign across the field, heading down to a stile and yellow waymark. Climb the stile, continue straight across the middle of the next field – there is no clear path, dropping sharply downhill and veering slightly left to climb another waymarked stile. Continue downhill, crossing a track by a finger-post, to the bottom left-hand corner of the field where there are two stiles. Turn left over the nearer stile and walk across a field, heading for a stile in the far right-hand corner.

Turn right over the stile, immediately cross a brook and then turn left **E** to join a broad woodland track after a few yards. Bear left and follow this track uphill through the woodlands of Weston Park, passing through a gate. Continue, now along the edge of a field with the woods on the left, go through another gate and keep ahead, climbing gently all the while and later passing through another gate to re-enter the woods, eventually reaching a lane **F**.

Turn left along this lane for ¼ mile (400m) to where it joins a main road and keep ahead for another ¼ mile (400m) to where the road bends slightly to the left. Here, at a Cotswold Way sign **G**, pick up a path that runs parallel to the road along the edge of a field. Soon there is a fine view of Chipping Campden down in the valley. After a while the path bears right, heading downhill in the direction of the church, to rejoin the road **H**. Turn right back into the town centre. ●

The glorious view from Dover's Hill

Wychwood Forest

Start	Charlbury
Distance	7 miles (11.25km)
Approximate time	4 hours
Parking	Charlbury
Refreshments	Pubs at Charlbury, pub at Finstock
Ordnance Survey maps	Landranger 164 (Oxford) and Pathfinder 1091, SP 21/31 (Burford & Witney (North))

For many years public access to Wychwood Forest was forbidden and its sylvan charms were hidden from view. Fortunately a waymarked 1½-mile (2.5km) route through it has now been opened up, forming the highlight of a pleasantly varied walk in the gently rolling country of the Evenlode valley. As well as the forest, the walk includes an attractive old town, deer park and extensive views across farmland to the hills beyond.

The quiet town of Charlbury has a fine situation on the slopes of the Evenlode valley, overlooking the expanses of Wychwood Forest on the western slopes. It was once noted for its glove-making industry and has a number of old houses dating back to the 16th and 17th centuries. Dominating the town is the tower of its medieval church.

Begin at the top end of Church Street by taking the road signposted to Chipping Norton and Burford. Turn left down Dyers Hill and follow the road for ½ mile (800m) out of the town, over the River Evenlode and over the railway. About 200 yds (184m) past the railway bridge turn right **A**, at a bridleway and Oxfordshire Way sign, along a tarmac drive to Walcot Farm. Continue, passing cottages on the right, along the bridleway to Chilson, which is now a broad track, for nearly 1 mile (1.5km) to go through a metal gate and on to a lane **B**. Turn left along the lane for 1¼ miles (2km), keeping ahead over the B4437 to enter Wychwood Forest.

The present forest is but a remnant of the vast medieval royal hunting ground that once extended over much of western Oxfordshire and was a favourite with Norman kings. A number of deer parks were carved from the forest, including Cornbury and Blenheim, and over the years it became progressively reduced in size and was finally disafforested in 1856.

Bear right at a junction **C** and walk along the lane to a waymarked stile and 'Circular Walk' footpath sign on the left **D**. Climb the stile to follow a route well waymarked with yellow-topped posts and white plastic markers through the forest for the next 1½ miles (2.5km) along undulating paths and broad rides, through beautiful woodland and grassy glades. After crossing the end of a narrow lake on the right, turn sharp left **E**, still following the waymarked route, and head up to a stile. Climb over and keep ahead to soon emerge from the trees, continuing along a path, at first by the side of woodland on the

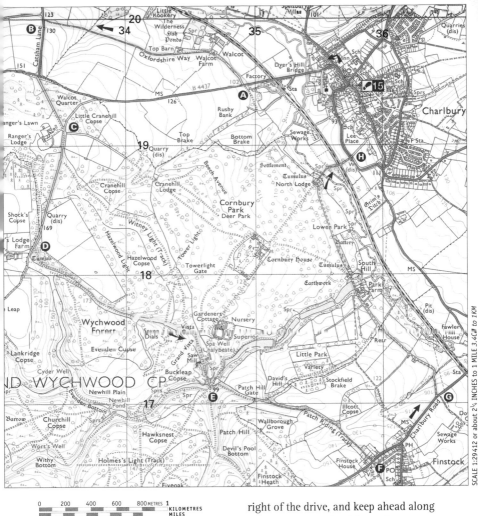

SCALE 1:29,412 or about 2¼ INCHES to 1 MILE 3.4⊠ to 1KM

left, later across fields and finally between cottages, to reach a road almost opposite Finstock's small 19th-century church **F**.

Turn left along the road – passing a road on the right that leads to the pub and Finstock village – for ½ mile (800m), turning left along a tarmac drive at a 'Circular Walk' sign **G**. Keep along this tree-lined track for nearly 1½ miles (2.5km) as you pass through Cornbury Park, a 600-acre (268 ha) deer park originally carved from Wychwood Forest. Soon after passing the end of a lake on the left, go through a white gate with a footpath sign to the

right of the drive, and keep ahead along the right-hand side of the park boundary fence, with woodland on the right and fine views across the deer park to the left. Continue over four stiles, finally going through a metal gate by a handsome lodge and keeping ahead a few yards to a door with a footpath sign on it. Go through that to turn right along the broad drive of Cornbury Park – to the left are the entrance gates and a glimpse of the 17th-century mansion.

Cross the River Evenlode and the railway, continue to a road and turn left **H** into Charlbury, making for the church. Turn right by the church up the broad, handsome Church Street back to the starting point. ●

Cooper's Hill and Buckholt Wood

Start	Cooper's Hill
Distance	5½ miles (8.75km)
Approximate time	3 hours
Parking	Cooper's Hill picnic area
Refreshments	Pub at Cranham, tea-rooms at Cooper's Hill
Ordnance Survey maps	Landrangers 162 (Gloucester and Forest of Dean) and 163 (Cheltenham & Cirencester), Pathfinder 1089, SO 81/91 (Gloucester & Birdlip)

Cooper's Hill is one of a series of vantage points on the Cotswold escarpment and the views from it westwards – looking across the Vale of Severn to Gloucester Cathedral – are outstanding. It is also situated amidst some of the most extensive areas of woodland in the Cotswolds, especially the beautiful Cranham Woods that lie to the south and east. The walk begins by exploring parts of this woodland and later passes close to a Roman villa before ascending the hill, noted for its 'cheese-rolling' competitions. Finally it descends via more woodland to the starting point.

Begin at the car park by going through a yellow arrowed gate by the side of the public conveniences into Upton Wood, one of a series of adjacent woods, usually known collectively as Cranham Woods. Immediately turn right at a 'Nature Trail' sign, bear left up some steps and at the top turn right along a broad woodland path **A**. Continue along this path, ignoring all side paths, as it curves to the left uphill and becomes narrower. Just after passing a notice-board for Buckholt Wood National Nature Reserve bear left at a fork and head downhill to a lane. Buckholt Wood is another part of Cranham Woods. Cross the lane and continue ahead, bearing slightly left to pass to the left of another notice-board. At a fork, keep along the right-hand

path, heading downhill to the edge of the wood and on to another lane **B**.

Turn left downhill into Cranham village and continue uphill to a road junction **C**. The village is small but scattered and the mainly 15th-century church lies nearly ¾ mile (1.25km) away across Cranham Common. At the junction turn left, at a footpath sign, along a track and at the first fork continue along the left-hand track, soon re-entering Buckholt Wood. Following a well-waymarked route, cross a stream and head uphill, passing a house on the right and continuing along a tarmac drive to a road **D**. Turn left and at a footpath sign turn right along a track by the right-hand edge of the wood. Head downhill and after passing another nature reserve notice-

Buckholt Wood

board keep ahead at a fork. On meeting another track, bear left and follow it along the edge of the wood, in the direction of more yellow arrows, re entering the wood where the track bends right to a fork **E**.

At this point you can make a slight detour to visit Witcombe Roman Villa. Follow the right-hand fork downhill, go through a metal gate and keep along the top edge of a field. Climb a stile and passing to the right of Cooper's Hill Farm continue along a tarmac drive, turning right down to the villa. It was built towards the end of the 1st century AD and a small building on the site houses a mosaic pavement depicting fishes and other sea creatures, and other objects found during excavation.

To continue the walk from **E**, at the fork take the left-hand uphill track, at first through Cooper's Hill Wood. Later the track curves to the left along the edge of the wood steadily climbing. Go through a gate, after which the track becomes a narrow tarmac lane, continuing through the hamlet of Cooper's Hill. Turn left, following a Cotswold Way sign, into a small car park **G** and bear right to a kissing-gate in some trees. Go through and walk along a wooded uphill path, turning left at a fork and following yellow arrows steeply uphill to the left, emerging on to an open grassy clearing where there is a tall maypole. This is where the annual 'cheese-rolling' competitions begin. They are held on Spring Bank Holiday Monday, along with other fairly robust events at the same time.

At the maypole turn right along a grassy path downhill through Brockworth Wood, turning left at a T-junction of paths. Climb a stile and bear left, soon bearing right at a fork and heading gently downhill. Continue through woodland to the top of some steps **A**, rejoining the outward route, turning right to return to the car park. ●

Wotton-under-Edge, the Tyndale Monument and Coombe Hill

Start	Wotton-under-Edge
Distance	5½ miles (8.75km)
Approximate time	3½ hours
Parking	Chipping Car Park, Wotton-under-Edge
Refreshments	Pubs and cafés in Wotton-under-Edge, pubs at North Nibley, pub at Waterley Bottom
Ordnance Survey maps	Landranger 162 (Gloucester & Forest of Dean) and Pathfinder 1132, ST 69/79 (Dursley & Wotton-under-Edge)

This walk leads to two of the western outliers of the Cotswolds from where the views to the west from Nibley Knoll and to the south from Coombe Hill are wonderful. The walking is varied and interesting and do not be put off by the amount of road walking on the return leg; the lane is quiet and the countryside beautiful as it winds past farms and cottages.

Wotton's name clearly reveals its geographical position – under the edge, or at the foot of the Cotswold escarpment. Its many fine houses from the 16th, 17th and 18th centuries reflect the town's former importance and prosperity as a centre for the cloth trade, as does the 15th-century church, which has a superb Perpendicular tower, and the Georgian town hall.

The walk begins in Tabernacle Street at the top end of Bear Street. The distinctive Tabernacle Church now serves a new purpose as auction rooms. Climb up the road in front of the church, ignoring the footpath sign to the right of the building, pass the long graveyard and carry straight on past the dead-end sign. This leads to a narrow footpath which climbs to a lane where there is a convenient seat to admire the view for those who wish to rest after the short climb. Continue up the lane and after 300 yds (274m) take the waymarked path over the stile on the left for Wotton Hill. The path winds through the woods, roughly parallel to the road, climbing all the while. Leave the woods by crossing over a stile to reach a circular wall which encloses a clump of trees. A notice here says that trees were planted here to commemorate Waterloo.

'They had become thin by the end of the Crimean War and were felled for a bonfire. This walled enclosure was erected and trees planted to commemorate the Jubilee of Her late Majesty Queen Victoria (1887) following the burning in this spot of one of a chain of celebration beacons which then spanned the country. It was

SCALE 1:25000 or 2½ INCHES to 1 MILE 4CM to 1KM

0	200	400	600	800 METRES	**1**	
0	200	400	600 YARDS		**½**	KILOMETRES MILES

interplanted with new trees in 1952.' None of the trees look too healthy now, but they still serve as a landmark on the top of Wotton Hill **A**, on the western flank of the Cotswolds.

Leave the circular wall and climb up to the stile. Follow the field edge with the trees on the left and soon the yellow-waymarked path enters Westridge Wood, a National Trust

property. Bear left where the path divides, on rough granite chippings which look as though they may have been reclaimed from a redundant railway track. The granite makes the path easily distinguishable but the walking is rough. The path divides once more: keep right this time, then right again. A tower becomes visible through the trees on the left – this is the monument on Nibley Knoll **B**.

At last the path emerges from the wood and the memorial can now be seen at the far end of the meadow ahead. It was erected in 1866 to the memory of William Tyndale, 'Translator of the English Bible who first caused the New Testament to be printed in the mother tongue of his countrymen. Born near this spot he suffered martyrdom at Vilvorde in Flanders on October 6th, 1536.'

The views from here are even better than those from Wotton Hill. On a clear day the Welsh hills are easily visible beyond the twin piers of the Severn Bridge. A bronze plaque helps to identify the various landmarks.

From the monument keep the woods on the left and before the quarry enter them over a stile. Bear right on to a sunken lane and at the top bear left into the trees, following a path downhill. This soon descends steeply down the flank of the hill to another stile at the bottom. Keep the hedge on the right to find a stile on to a lane at the bottom of the field and turn right.

Little traffic passes along this byway and the walking is pleasant. Bear right at the telephone-box at Pitt Court, heading for Waterley Bottom. After about ½ mile (800m) bear left if you need food or drink at the New Inn, a wonderfully remote hostelry, returning to the main route afterwards by bearing left at the junction and then right at Brookside Cottage.

Otherwise continue along the lane, turning right at Brookside Cottage, towards Wotton, along a very narrow enclosed lane with steep banks. Look for Apple Tree Farm on the right: soon after it a bridleway forks off on the left **Ⓒ**. Take this steep and enclosed bridleway, a very ancient track, which briefly enters a wood. Cross the road at the top, walk along a short stretch enclosed by hedges and climb the stile on the right where the path to the left plunges downhill **Ⓓ**.

This path follows the contours just below the summit of Coombe Hill, with the village nestling below. The path follows round the head of the coombe, the name of which recalls the *cwm* in the names of Welsh mountains. Keep to the right where the path divides, with a fence on the right, and climb a stile. Just as the path meets the wood take a footpath on the left, by making a hairpin turn, down through the trees. Fork right before a stile to descend steeply – the wooden steps are a great help here – to another stile by a house which has a fine garden. Turn left on to the road and after walking for 50 yds (46m) turn right and climb over a stile. Keep the hedge on the right to find a path at the bottom of the field. The spire of the Tabernacle Church now comes into view ahead, and this footpath leads down to the side of it and thus back to the starting point. ●

The Tyndale Monument

Haresfield Beacon and Standish Wood

Start	Shortwood car park, on minor road between Painswick and Haresfield
Distance	7 miles (11.25km)
Approximate time	3½ hours
Parking	National Trust car park at Shortwood
Refreshments	Pub at Randwick
Ordnance Survey maps	Landranger 162 (Gloucester & Forest of Dean) and Pathfinder 1113, SO 80/90 (Stroud)

There can be no denying that the first leg of this route is the most spectacular – on a clear day the views go on forever. The rest of the walk has many fine moments; in winter the trees on the woodland section provide shelter from the wind and there are several short climbs to keep the circulation moving.

The National Trust has a notice-board in its car park at Shortwood which gives background information on Haresfield Beacon and on Standish Wood, which the last part of the walk passes through.

Leave the car park and head across the grass to the topograph viewpoint, which is clearly signposted **Ⓐ**. The Shortwood topograph is a remarkable work of art executed in bronze, which displays the local countryside in miniature. The hills are contoured and roads and rivers shown. On a good day it is possible to see the Sugar Loaf Mountain in South Wales, more than 30 miles (48km) away.

Turn back after admiring the view, keeping along the right-hand edge of the woodland, and at the end of the field by the wall there is a waymark. Bear left here through the trees, following the wall on the right. The path descends to a stile; climb over and at a fork a little further on bear right

along the upper path, following yellow waymarks up some steps and on to a lane. Turn left at the Cotswold Way sign – there is also a National Trust sign for Haresfield Beacon just ahead, go through a gate and keep by a wire fence on the right to a stile. Climb over and continue ahead, negotiating the prominent earthworks of the Iron Age fort, to the triangulation pillar at Haresfield Beacon **Ⓑ**. Again, the view across the Vale of Gloucester looking towards the Forest of Dean and mountains of South Wales is magnificent and it is no wonder that such a fine vantage point above steep slopes should have been utilised as a defensive position by both prehistoric peoples and the Romans.

At the triangulation pillar turn sharp right, almost doubling back, and make for a stile by a line of trees on the left. Climb over and walk along a path, between a wire fence on the right and wooded slopes on the left, later

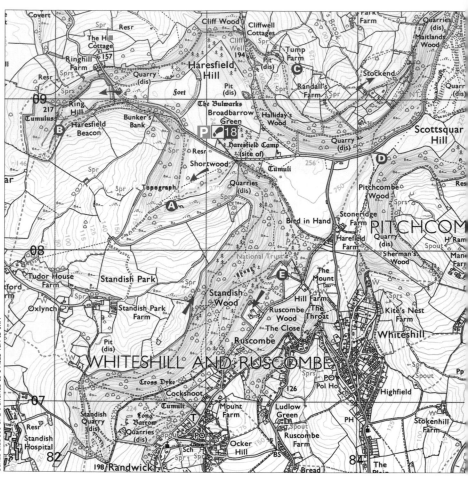

SCALE 1:25000 or 2½ INCHES to 1 MILE 4CM to 1KM

```
0    200   400   600   800 METRES  1
                                      KILOMETRES
                                      MILES
0    200   400   600 YARDS    ½
```

continuing down a farm track and through a metal gate on to a lane.

Turn left to walk along the lane and then immediately right to leave it, on the bridleway signposted Cotswold Way and Edge and Painswick. There is easy walking now through the woods following a blue waymark. At the top stands a curious granite memorial which commemorates the ending of the siege of Gloucester by Royalist forces in 1643. The well-maintained bridleway descends to a lane, passing on the way a quaint well which is inscribed with the following verse:

✠ *Deo Gratias*
Whoever the Bucketfull upwindeth
Let him bless God, who Water findeth
Yet Water here but small availeth
Go seek that Well which never faileth.

Turn right at the lane and then left down a steep track to Tump Farm **C**. Turn right at the farm gate over a stile and cross the field, with the farm on the left, to a gate in the bottom left corner. Bear right after this to find a stile to the right of a clump of lime trees at the bottom. The path winds through two more fields with woods on the right to emerge on the driveway of Randall's Farm. Turn right along the drive and where it meets the woods again take the path to the right into the woods following a waymark on a telephone pole. It is a dark, narrow and underused path which meanders up past an unusual clump of young yews, continuing past the group of cottages at Stockend, where it becomes quite difficult and overgrown.

Turn right where the path meets a track and follow this for about 500 yds (457m), looking for a path leading off to the left into the woods. This climbs steeply up the valley to meet a road at the top **D**. Cross the road to a field path opposite and walk over the meadow, heading just to the right of the house on the far side. Turn to the left on to the road here and then right on to the lane to Randwick. Follow this to Park Bungalow where you turn sharply to the right into Standish Wood. The path soon forks left to pass behind the bungalow. Another path joins from the right: keep to the left as you descend through trees, following a yellow waymark down the main drive which drops down to pine trees. Here **E** there

Triangulation pillar at Haresfield Beacon

is a choice. There are paths to the right which lead down through the woods to the western path at the bottom – then you have to climb again to reach the starting point at Shortwood. The longer alternative, which the main route follows, continues by forking left after the pines, following the yellow waymarks. Pass through the gate at the bottom, turn left and then left again to reach the road, and turn right into Randwick village. There is a pub – the Vine Tree Inn – just beyond the telephone box.

At a footpath sign about 100 yds (92m) before the pub, turn right along a path to reach the woods again, bearing right on to the main path. This leads to a major path junction. Bear slightly to the right here to cross the major path to reach a fence crossed by a stile. Turn to the left after climbing over the stile, and then right at another footpath crossroads. This descends steeply to reach the main track through the western side of the woods. Turn right on to this and after about 30 minutes' walking, and a final steep climb, you return to the starting point. ●

Adlestrop, Cornwell and Oddington

Start	Adlestrop
Distance	8 miles (12.75km)
Approximate time	4 hours
Parking	Village hall car park at Adlestrop
Refreshments	Pub at Lower Oddington
Ordnance Survey maps	Landranger 163 (Cheltenham & Cirencester), Pathfinder 1068, SP 22/32 (Chipping Norton & Adlestrop)

The Evenlode is one of a number of small rivers that cut delightful valleys as they flow leisurely south-eastwards from the Cotswolds to the Oxford Plain and the Thames. Much of this walk is in the Evenlode valley – through a quiet, largely unchanged area, with a surprisingly remote feel, on the Gloucestershire–Oxfordshire border – and it includes five less well-known villages, some superb churches and an optional visit to a fine 17th-century mansion.

Yes I remember Adlestrop –
The name, because one afternoon
Of heat the express train drew up there
Unwontedly. It was late June.

The steam hissed. Someone cleared his
* throat.*
No one left and no one came
On the bare platform. What I saw
Was Adlestrop – only the name.

Edward Thomas' poem, written just before World War I, immortalised the name of this tiny Cotswold village, as well as vividly evoking the heyday of rural railways, when even small, remote villages like this were linked to the outside world without losing their tranquillity or sense of remoteness. Adlestrop could hardly be more perfect – golden stone cottages, many of them thatched, situated close to the great house which dates mainly from the 16th to the 18th century, the whole of this

gentle and old-fashioned scene presided over by a medieval church.

Turn left out of the car park and almost immediately left again, at a public footpath sign. To the right is a small shelter which houses the old station nameplate – placed here, after the station was closed in the 1960s, as a tribute to Edward Thomas, one of the war poets, killed in action in 1917. Walk along a track which keeps by the right-hand edge of a field, by a hedge on the right; climb a stile and bear slightly left across the next field – there is no obvious path – making for the far left-hand corner. Here go through a gate and on to a waymarked gate on the left a few yards ahead. Go through that, turn right and keep along the edge of a field, by a hedge on the right, to go through a metal gate. Continue in a straight line across the next field, heading uphill to a yellow-waymarked gate on the wooded ridge in front. Turn round and look back at this point for a lovely view of Adlestrop lying below you. Go through the gate, keep ahead between trees for a few yards and then continue straight across the middle of a field, making for the end of a line of trees on the right. Over the crest of the hill there is a fine view to the left looking north-westwards.

At the far end of the field look out for a metal gate with a blue waymark; go through it and turn right **Ⓐ** on to a grassy path on the edge of the woods to the right. To the left there is an exquisite view across the field of Chastleton House and church standing side by side – unfortunately there is no public right of way to give direct access, so it is necessary to make a detour along a lane. Pass through a gate to enter Peasewell Wood, following a narrow but well-marked path through the trees, to reach a lane. Bear left for a few yards to where the lane bends sharply to the left **Ⓑ**.

Here you can continue along the lane for a 1-mile (1.5km) detour in order to make a visit to Chastleton House, a fine, unspoilt, Jacobean mansion which has an impressive south front. It was built by a local wool merchant in the early 17th century who purchased the estate from Robert Catesby of Gunpowder Plot fame. Inside it has fine panelling and furniture and its most outstanding features are the Great Hall and the Long Gallery on the top floor, which has a magnificent ceiling. The combination of great house, small village and simple church (dating back to Norman times) in close proximity could not be more attractive or traditional.

Return to the bend in the lane and at a bridleway sign to Cornwell turn left (or right if omitting the detour to Chastleton) through a gate. Immediately turn right through another gate and

then bear left to head across a field dotted at random with trees, keeping parallel to a wall on the right, beyond which is the lane. Head for a metal gate at the far end of the field, and when you reach it, go through and turn left for a few yards along a farm track. Then turn right through the first metal gate on the right and continue through two more gates, heading straight across to the Iron Age fort of Chastleton Barrow. Pass through the middle of the circular wooded enclosure to a metal gate at the far side, go through and continue along the edge of a field, by a hedge on the left, down to a road. Cross over and walk down the narrow lane directly opposite into the village of Cornwell, a distance of nearly ¾ mile (1.25km).

The lane curves gently right through the village but a detour to the left, along a track marked 'To the Church', through a gate, then turning right along the right-hand edge of a field, brings you past the back of the mainly 18th-century manor house and down to the delightful little church, a plain, simple building with a bell-tower, which retains some original Norman arches. After returning from this brief detour, walk through the village to a road **Ⓒ**. Many of the buildings of Cornwell, including the manor house, were restored or smartened in the late 1930s

Adlestrop

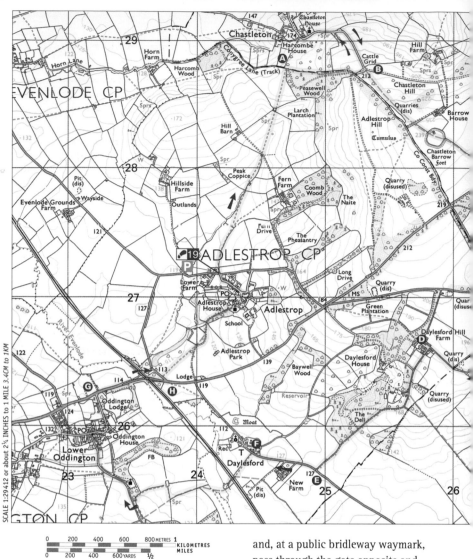

SCALE 1:29412 or about 2¼ INCHES to 1 MILE 3.4CM to 1KM

0 200 400 600 800 METRES 1
0 200 400 600 YARDS ½
KILOMETRES
MILES

and early 1940s by a wealthy American lady who bought the estate. She employed the well-known Welsh architect Clough Williams-Ellis, renowned for his Italian-style village of Portmeirion in North Wales.

Cross the road and continue along the track straight ahead, following it as it turns right, passing a house on the left and then keeping ahead, past farm buildings on the left, to a gate. Go through and continue, gently climbing to the right-hand corner of a wood and on to go through a gate. Cross a lane

and, at a public bridleway waymark, pass through the gate opposite and slightly to the left, continuing along the very attractive path ahead, which skirts woodland on the right and has fine and extensive views to the left. The path drops down to join a broad track: turn right along it up to Daylesford Hill Farm and follow it as it turns left between the farm buildings **D**.

Keep along it for the next ¾ mile (1.25km) – the grounds of Daylesford House lie on the other side of the wall on the right but the house, the home of Warren Hastings, first governor general of India, remains well hidden by trees. Bear right at a fork, keeping by a high

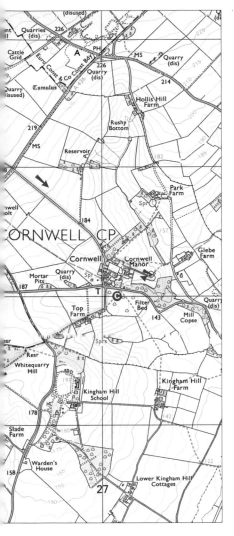

cross a footbridge over the little River Evenlode. Bear right across a field to go through a gate, continue along the edge of the next field to its top end and then go through a gap in the hedge on the right. Now turn right and follow the edge of the next field, turning left at the end of it and keeping along the edge up to a line of trees in front, where you turn right along a track.

On the right you soon pass Oddington church, a 13th- to 14th-century building with a fine Norman doorway. Its most unusual feature is the 14th-century Doom painting on the north wall of the nave, its gruesome details revealing much about medieval thought. Continue along what is now a tarmac lane into Lower Oddington, turn right at a T-junction and then follow the village street round to the left, passing Oddington House and the Fox Inn, up to the main road **G**. Turn right along the road for nearly ½ mile (800m), crossing the river and railway bridge, to the left of which stood the station where Edward Thomas saw 'Adlestrop – the name' when his train 'drew up there unwontedly'.

After crossing the bridge turn left for a few yards along the road which is signposted to Adlestrop and Evenlode **H**, and at a footpath sign on the right climb a stile, and another one a few yards ahead, and then head in a straight line across the grassland of Adlestrop Park in the direction of the large house in front. On meeting a track, bear left along it and follow its route around the right-hand edge of a cricket field and on to go through a gate which bears a blue waymark. Take the track ahead, which has wooden fences on both sides, to reach another gate. Go through this and keep ahead, with the house on the left and church on the right, into Adlestrop and through the village, finally returning to the car park. ●

wall on the right, and ignoring the yellow waymarks to the left continue gently downhill – with fine views over the Evenlode valley ahead – and by woodlands on the right, to a road **E**. Turn right along the road for just over ¼ mile (400m) towards the small estate village of Daylesford, dominated by its fine Victorian church which contains a monument to Warren Hastings.

On the edge of the village, turn left **F**, at a footpath sign to Oddington, through a gate and along a grassy path beside a field, by a wire fence and hedge on the right. Continue over the railway bridge down to a gate, go through it and across the field ahead to

Bath and Claverton Down

Start	Bath Abbey
Distance	8½ miles (13.5km)
Approximate time	4 hours
Parking	Bath
Refreshments	Pubs, restaurants and cafés in Bath, pub at Bathampton
Ordnance Survey maps	Landranger 172 (Bristol & Bath) and Pathfinder 1183, ST 66/76 (Bath & Keynsham)

At their southern end the Cotswolds descend abruptly to the Avon valley and the city of Bath, its elegant Georgian terraces and crescents rising up the steep slopes, giving the city its distinctive appearance. The walk reveals how quickly you can leave the city, by following the towpath of the Kennet and Avon Canal in a semi-circular loop around Bath's northern and eastern fringes. The route keeps along the canal as far as Claverton, then crosses Claverton Down to Sham Castle before dropping back to the city centre.

The walk begins in the abbey churchyard in the heart of Bath where the main stages in its history coalesce: the Roman baths, the Georgian grandeur of the Pump Room, the medieval abbey and the evidence of Bath's present-day popularity as a tourist centre. Walk past the north side of the abbey, keep ahead and turn left along Grand Parade above the River Avon on the right. Turn right over Pulteney Bridge, built by Robert Adam in 1770, and continue along Argyle Street and Great Pulteney Street. At the end bear left into Sydney Place, bear right up Beckford Road, and cross the railway bridge. Turn left on to the towpath of the Kennet and Avon Canal **A**. You keep along this for the next 3½ miles (5.5km) as it curves through the Avon valley around the edge of the city.

After nearly 1½ miles (2.5km) you reach Bathampton **B**. Continue along the canal for another 2 miles (3.5km) as it curves gently to the right all the time between the steep-wooded slopes of

Bathampton and later Hengrove Woods on the right, and the fields and hills of the Avon valley on the left.

You finally leave the towpath by an information board about Claverton Pumping Station **C**; you can make a brief detour to visit this by turning sharp left down a lane and over the railway to the river. The route continues by keeping ahead along the lane, following it to the right over a bridge and up to the main road. Turn right for 50 yds (46m) and just before a bus stop turn left **D** through a metal kissing-gate and along a path, by a wall on the left, into the village of Claverton. Ahead is the medieval church, heavily restored in the Victorian era.

Turn left through the village and at a T-junction turn right **E** along an uphill lane which threads through woodland. A few yards after passing the entrance to the American Museum, turn right through a gate in a hedge **F** and walk along a wooded uphill path. Cross a car park, bear right along a track and just in front of a

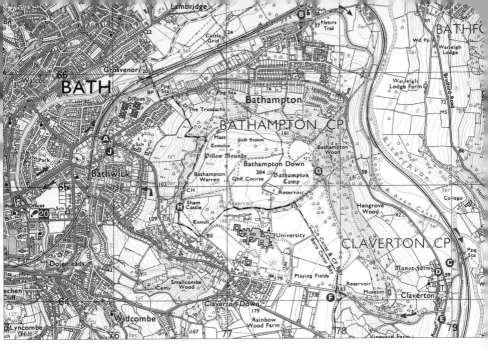

gate turn left through a gap in a hedge on to the edge of the university playing fields. Ahead are the modern buildings of Bath University.

Proceed over Claverton Down by turning right along a path, by a hedge on the right and passing a rifle range on the left, until you reach a stone stile. Climb over it to enter the National Trust property of Bushey Norwood and, following public footpath signs, continue along the edge of a field, by a wire fence on the right. Keep along the field edge, following the wire fence round to the right – there are good views now through gaps in the woods on the right across the Avon valley again – and at the end of the field go through a metal kissing-gate, at a public footpath sign.

Continue ahead for a few yards and turn left **G** at a path junction to soon emerge on to the corner of a golf course. Continue along the edge of the course, by a wall, trees and later the university buildings on the left, passing two bridleway signs to North Road. At the second sign keep ahead, ignoring its directions, still along the edge of the golf-course, following it round to the right to a public footpath to Sham Castle. Here bear slightly left along a path which heads gently downhill, passing the golf-club car park on the right, and turn left in front of Sham Castle **H**, a 19th-century folly. From here the unexpected view over the city, with the southern rim of the Cotswolds to the right, is magnificent.

With your back to Sham Castle, and slightly to the right of it, take a wooded downhill path which bears left to a drive. Cross over, go through a kissing-gate opposite and continue more steeply downhill to a stile and on to a road. Turn right for 200 yds (184m), turn left through a kissing-gate and along a downhill path, by a wire fence on the left, through another kissing-gate and ahead between walls to another road. Cross over, continue along the road opposite, Sham Castle Road, and turn right at the end of it up to a main road **J**. Turn left, cross the canal and railway and retrace your steps, via Sydney Gardens and Great Pulteney Street, to the starting point by the abbey. ●

Laurie Lee Country

Laurie Lee Country

Start	Slad
Distance	7 miles (11.25km) Shorter version 5½ miles (8.75km)
Approximate time	4½ hours (3 hours for shorter version)
Parking	Small area beside a byway in centre of Slad, by a notice board, or at Bulls Cross, just before **G**. If latter is used, the full walk must be followed
Refreshments	Pub in Slad
Ordnance Survey maps	Landrangers 162 (Gloucester & Forest of Dean) and 163 (Cheltenham & Cirencester) and Pathfinder 1113, SO 80/90 (Stroud)

The western Cotswolds have many valleys that seem almost private, completely hidden off the beaten track. This walk leads to one of these, concealed by hill contours and dense woods. The route may look easy, but the gradients are often severe and the going sometimes difficult. Slad and the valleys around are closely identified with the author Laurie Lee; his book Cider with Rosie *is set in the area.*

From the parking area continue down the byway and turn to the right after the Old House. At the bottom of the hill, just beyond the big house on the right, turn to the right by a pond **A**; a yellow arrow on a telephone-pole opposite points the way. Climb a stile and, keeping a hedge on the right, climb another stile into the wood and zigzag up a steep bank to reach a wall at the top. Turn left, follow the path alongside the wall, and turn right at a crossways to follow a sunken track up through fine beeches. Just beyond an overgrowing yew tree turn sharply left on to a higher track which soon emerges on to the edge of the wood, allowing views of the valley below.

Continue along this delightful route for almost 1 mile (1.5km), keeping to the main path along the edge of the woods. At one point paths leave to left and right but the route continues ahead. Soon after this, just before an iron gate,

the path swings left **B** and becomes narrow and muddy as it descends steeply to the floor of the valley. Cross the stream and climb the other side of the valley to reach a path below some cottages. Turn right on to this and then sharp left to pass behind the cottages, walking on a concrete track which soon swings to the right, to reach another cottage.

Take the second path on the left on this hairpin bend. This swings sharply to the right and descends, giving views into another valley. A path joins from the left after the descent, and a few yards after this there are steps on the left **C** which take a narrow

path down to the edge of the trees. Cross the stile here and turn right into a meadow. Another stile takes the path into woodland again, and a section of more difficult walking follows as the path clings to the steep-sided slopes above the stream. An overhead electric wire heralds the end of this section where the path passes through a gate at the end of the meadow.

Turn left on to a narrow enclosed path which leads down to an isolated cottage. Pass to the right of this and climb a steep path. The stile on the left offers a less demanding, less scenic route which follows the drive from the farm on the other side of the valley. Our route continues up the steep path which joins a track well used by riders. It passes some posts of a disused boundary fence – there is a cottage on the right – and 200 yds (183m) further on swings to the right and begins to climb steeply. Turn off to the left here on a faint path to descend to a new stile at the bottom of the wood. Bear right in the meadow, heading towards a field opening with a cattle-trough close by **D**. The gatepost here is marked with a yellow direction arrow; follow this to the left to pick up a track, leaving it before reaching the farm, at a post on the left which bears a direction arrow pointing to the right. This leads into the woods, to a fence at a higher level and a stile which crosses it. The path now climbs steeply through the trees, crossing a track and continuing upwards until it reaches a stone stile, where it leads into a field. Follow the edge of this field for about 100 yds (92m) to reach the track that leads to Down Barn Farm.

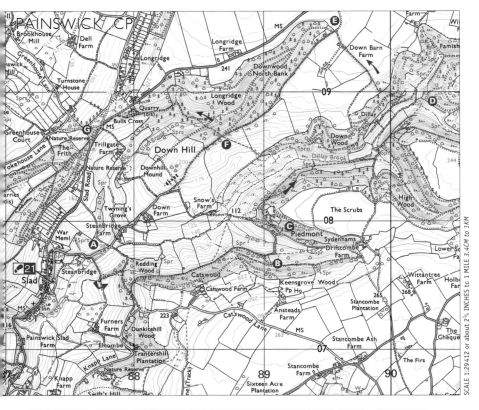

This is easy, level walking. Pass the farm and then take the track to the left **E**. After a further easy, pleasant stretch through trees for about 20 minutes, the trees thin on the right, allowing lovely views down into Slad. The side of the valley crossed in the initial stage of the walk can also be clearly seen. As the track begins to descend look for a clearing on the right, with a red gate into the forest, and a stone stile on the other side of the track a little further down **F**.

For the shorter version, continue along the track which begins a steady descent and soon becomes a metalled lane. After passing Down and Steanbridge farms, the lane brings us back to the Old House at Slad; bear left to retrace your steps and return to the starting point.

Take a faint path directly opposite the stone stile which leads off to the right at 45°. This descends steeply but soon comes to a more distinct path. Follow this to the bottom, crossing another track *en route*. There is a lovely

pond on the right as the path now climbs up to a track on the other side of the valley. Turn left on to this and climb steadily up to the road.

Turn left at the road and admire the view of Painswick through the trees. After the road junctions to Sheepscombe and Painswick on the right, take the bridleway on the right, by the bus stop, into Frith Wood Nature Reserve **G**. The track climbs steeply through a wood of tall beeches, keeping near the edge of the wood to a gate at the end.

Go through the gate, climb a stile, continue down the farm track and pass through the farmyard on to a made-up road. At the end of the wood on the left turn left over a stile. This is Folly Acres Conservation Area, the 'Rural Conservation and Organic Growing Study Centre to promote The Organic Management of Land'. Keep the wall and the wood on the left to drop down to the track which leads to the main road. Where the track divides take the footpath on the right to reach the road. Turn left into Slad, passing the small 19th-century church. ●

The village of Slad and Downhill Mound

Stanton, Stanway and Snowshill

Start	Stanton
Distance	8 miles (12.75km)
Approximate time	5½ hours
Parking	Stanton
Refreshments	Pub at Stanton, pub at Snowshill
Ordnance Survey maps	Landranger 150 (Worcester & The Malverns), Pathfinder 1043, SP 03/13 (Broadway & Chipping Campden)

This is a delightful route, with excellent walking interspersed with features of historic and architectural interest. Snowshill and Stanton are two of the loveliest Cotswold villages – views of the former can be enjoyed both on entering and leaving. The starting point, Stanton, snug in its valley and hidden by trees, reappears suddenly at the end, a wonderful surprise. The walk mainly follows the contours; there is only one stiffish climb – through Lidcombe Wood.

Stanton is a delightfully quiet and unspoilt village and the church is a lovely little building, of Norman origin but with a 15th-century tower and spire and some fine stained glass which came from Hailes Abbey. In springtime the verdant churchyard and the yellow of the laburnum at the gate make Stanton church one of the scenic gems of the Cotswolds.

Turn right out of the car park and at a T-junction right again, in the direction signposted to Stanway. Walk through the village until you see a distinctive lantern on the left. Take the footpath immediately after this; it is on the same side, signposted Cotswold Way **Ⓐ**. Pass Chestnut Farm and bear right out of the farmyard to a stile across the field. This path is well signposted and avoids steep gradients by following the contours through or by the side of fields, meadows and parkland. There are lovely vistas to the

west of hills, fields and woods. Almost too soon the path meets the driveway to Stanway House by a beautiful cricket ground. Stanway House, open on Tuesdays and Thursdays in June, July and August between 2 and 5pm, is a handsome 17th-century building surrounded by lovely gardens. In the grounds is a 14th-century tithe barn which once belonged to the monks of Tewksesbury Abbey.

Turn left to pass the house, tithe barn and church – the latter is more interesting from the outside although the interior is cool and peaceful. Note the unusual *memento mori* crucifix which is preserved in the south window of the chancel.

Pass in front of the wonderful gatehouse and turn left into the estate yard, following the footpath signs through an orchard. Turn left on to the road and after ¼ mile (400m), where the road bends sharply to the right, keep straight on, passing a dead-end sign and cottages **B**. There is a very faded signboard in property by the farmyard. Take the left fork here, for Shenberrow and Snowshill by Lidcombe Wood, and embark on the steepest climb of this walk, following blue arrows on green posts. Papermill Farm is in the lovely valley on the left, though this view is soon screened by trees as you enter Lidcombe Wood.

The path divides in a clearing: take the right fork to climb steeply up through the trees. It is a long climb to the gate at the top of the woods, where there is a footpath crossroads. Bear left on to the blue waymarked path across a field, turn left and then right at the next footpath junction and cross the field diagonally. Snowshill now comes into view below.

In the next field keep by the wall on the right to find a gate at the bottom. Bear right on to a lane which leads down to Oat Hill and Snowshill, a delightful village with houses and cottages grouped around the village green by the church.

Snowshill church is Victorian and replaced a tiny 13th-century chapel. Snowshill Manor is a most interesting and attractive Tudor building with later additions, standing in beautiful terraced gardens. It houses a large collection of items amassed by Charles Wade, its eccentric last owner, who gave it to the National Trust in 1951.

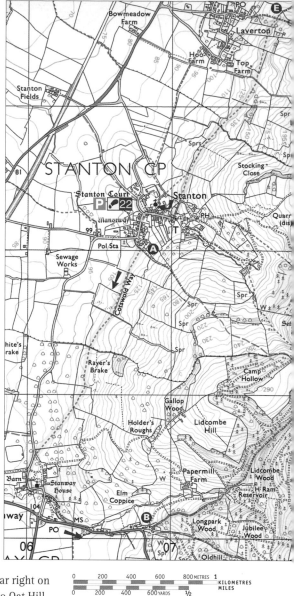

Retrace your steps back through the village and, just beyond Oat Hill Farm Hotel on the left, look out for a gate by a public footpath stone on the right **C**. Go through this and then proceed down a steep track until you reach the bottom of the valley; there is a pond on the right. At the bottom gate turn left, keeping a new hedge on the right, and descend to a stile at the bottom corner of the field. The path winds around the

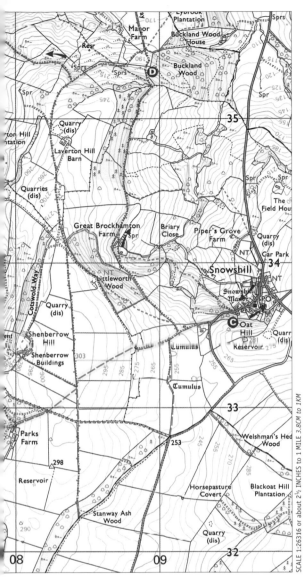

top, or far end, of the wood. Bear left here **D**, following the contours and keeping the wood on the left. From here the view is superb: Broadway to the right, the churches of Buckland and Childs Wickham clearly visible, and the Vale of Evesham beyond. Go through the gate at the bottom right corner of a field to follow a wire fence up to the corner of a small wood. Before reaching this coppice bear to the right to find a sunken track leading downhill.

Continue to descend, meeting another sunken track coming from the right. As Laverton comes into view below, look for a footpath sign **E**, on the left by some pollarded willows, pointing out the route which follows the flank of the hill.

Pass through the trees and over a stile into a meadow which was once farmed by the ridge and furrow, or strip cultivation, method. The path is very pleasant, easy and well-waymarked, following the contours closely and allowing you to enjoy lovely views over the vale as it passes through a succession of meadows. The spire of Stanton church comes into view quite suddenly. At a fork bear left, soon joining a farm track leading to the centre of the village. Turn right through the village, passing the church on the right, and right again to make your way back to the car park. ●

SCALE 1:26316 or about 2½ INCHES to 1 MILE 3.8CM to 1KM

shoulder of the hill, still following the line of the hedge.

Cross a stile and head just to the left of Great Brockhamton Farm, still following the contours. Pass through a gate and on to the farm drive; turn left, followed by a hairpin turn to the right up a made-up track, passing behind the farm. From here there are views of Broadway, overlooked by the tower on the shoulder of the hill opposite. On the left there is a plantation of young trees.

The track continues along the right-hand edge of woods to a gate at the

Winchcombe, Hailes Abbey and Sudeley Castle

Start	Winchcombe
Distance	8½ miles (13.5km)
Approximate time	4½ hours
Parking	Winchcombe
Refreshments	Pubs and cafés at Winchcombe
Ordnance Survey maps	Landrangers 150 (Worcester & The Malverns) and 163 (Cheltenham & Cirencester), Pathfinders 1067, SP 02/12 (Stow-on-the-Wold) and 1043, SP 03/13 (Broadway & Chipping Campden)

This is a fairly lengthy but relatively easy walk that combines splendid scenery with considerable historic appeal. Starting in one of the Cotswolds' most appealing small towns, it follows the Cotswold Way across fields to the attractively situated ruins of a 13th-century abbey, continues via a woodland path to the hamlet of Farmcote and then mainly follows lanes and tracks to a restored 15th-century manor house. From there it is just a short stroll back to the starting point.

There are virtually no visible remains of the powerful abbey that was responsible for much of Winchcombe's prosperity in the Middle Ages, bringing pilgrims into the town and developing the woollen industry. However, there is still plenty to remind us that Winchcombe was a flourishing Cotswold wool town: several attractive streets of stone and half-timbered buildings; the medieval George Inn, originally built as a guest house for pilgrims visiting the shrine of St Kenelm at the abbey; and a typical 15th-century 'wool church', financed jointly by local people, the abbot and Ralph Boteler, the builder of nearby Sudeley Castle. The church is distinguished by its imposing Perpendicular tower and fine spacious interior. Winchcombe's earlier history,

however, makes it more than just another wool town – it was one of the earliest Saxon boroughs, and during the early 11th century was even briefly the capital of its own shire, Wincelcumbeshire, before being annexed by Gloucestershire.

From the town centre walk northwards along High Street, passing the George Inn on the right, continue along Hailes Street (Broadway direction), cross the little River Isbourne, and shortly afterwards turn right, at a Cotswold Way sign **Ⓐ**, along Puck Pit Lane, a narrow tarmac lane. After a while the lane continues as a rough track, pleasantly hedge- and tree-lined; where that peters out continue over two stiles in quick succession, following yellow waymarks, and then bear slightly left to head diagonally across a field to a footbridge over a ditch. Cross it and continue ahead, climbing a slight rise and then dropping gently to go through a metal kissing-gate. The whole of this part of the route is well waymarked with Cotswold Way yellow arrows. Follow a path across the next field to pass through another metal kissing-gate, continue along the right-hand edge of a field for a few yards and then turn right over a stile. Bear slightly left to head straight across the next field, making for a post with a yellow arrow. Here bear right to continue along the left-hand edge of a field, by a hedge on the left, and at a T-junction turn left along a broad track, going through two gates and on to a lane **B**.

Turn right along the lane for a short distance, then turn left along a drive, passing houses on the right. Continue through a gate and straight across a field – there is a good view of the abbey ruins from here – making for a kissing-gate at the far end opposite Hailes church **C**. Go through and turn right along the lane up to the abbey.

Not much is left of Hailes Abbey apart from foundations and substantial parts of the cloisters, but the attractive and tranquil setting and the displays in the museum on the site partially

The ruins of Hailes Abbey

compensate for this. The Cistercian abbey was founded in 1246 by Richard, Earl of Cornwall, brother of Henry III, and quickly became prosperous, not just as a result of sheep farming but also through its possession of a phial supposedly of Christ's blood, a holy relic which made it a major centre for pilgrimage. The enormous length of the church (341ft/103m) is an indication of its great wealth, but as with all the other larger monasteries it was dissolved by Henry VIII in 1539. The tiny parish church just passed is also worth visiting for its medieval wall paintings and 15th-century rood screen, and for the contrast between its simplicity and the largely vanished opulence of the abbey.

Continue along the lane for ¼ mile (400m), and where it curves right to Hailes Fruit Farm keep ahead along a steadily ascending track by the right-hand edge of a wood. At a footpath sign continue straight ahead along the track, following directions to Farmcote, and with fields on both sides now there are fine open views, especially to the right. Keep climbing steadily to pass between farm buildings and on through a gate to a tarmac lane **D**. Continue along the lane through the hamlet of Farmcote, passing the tiny restored Norman church on the right. From this upland position there are excellent views to the right over the valley, looking towards Bredon Hill and the Malverns beyond.

Follow the lane for ¾ mile (1.25km), bearing right at a junction signposted to Winchcombe and Andoversford. Take the first turning on the left by some houses, at an 'Unsuitable for Motors'

notice, and at the end of farm buildings turn right through a metal gate with a bridleway sign and blue waymark **E**. Walk along the right-hand edge of a field, following it as it curves slightly to the left, with woodland on the right. Over to the left can be seen the large sylvan expanse of Guiting Wood. Continue through a metal gate and along the right-hand edge of the next field, climbing gently along an ancient pack-horse route called Campden Lane. Keep ahead, passing a house on the right, now along the left-hand edge of a field, finally following the track between trees and hedges – this last stretch can sometimes be overgrown – to a lane.

Turn left for 200 yds (184m) and where the lane starts to curve to the left turn right **F** on to a broad track, after a few yards turning right again along a narrow path – this is not very clear so keep a sharp eye out for it. The path heads through bushes for a few yards and then continues along the right-hand edge of a field, by a wood and later a wall on the right, to come out on to a narrow lane, the Salt Way, a section of another ancient routeway across the Cotswolds, linking the salt workings at Droitwich with the Thames valley. Turn left for a few yards and then turn right through a gate and along the drive to Parks Farm. From here there are glorious views ahead of rolling wooded hills and the buildings of Winchcombe, with the church tower dominant. Pass through a metal gate and continue, gently descending and curving right to a gate. Go through, keep ahead for a few yards and then turn sharp right **G**, above cottages and farm buildings on the left, passing through a metal gate and continuing along a winding and undulating farm road. Go through another metal gate, turn right through a gate, at a public

bridleway sign, to pass in front of the imposing 18th-century Sudeley Lodge; over to the left is the first view of Sudeley Castle, with the town of Winchcombe beyond.

About ¼ mile (400m) past the lodge, and just before another house on the right, turn left **H** off the drive at a footpath sign, go through a gate and head downhill along the right-hand edge of a field to a stile. Climb over, cross a ditch and turn right along the right-hand edge of the next field, with the castle directly ahead, following the field edge and a yellow waymark round to the left to climb another stile. Continue ahead a few yards to a stile in the hedge to the right, climb over, turn half-left and head diagonally across a large, sloping field – passing close to Sudeley Castle on the right – to a kissing-gate near the far right-hand corner. Go through and continue, keeping roughly parallel to a wire fence on the right, through two metal gates to come out on to the castle drive. Bear slightly left along the drive to return to Winchcombe; turn right if you wish to visit the castle.

Despite its name, Sudeley was actually a manor house rather than a castle proper because it lacked any serious fortifications. Originally built in the 15th century by Ralph Boteler, Admiral of the Fleet and first Baron Sudeley, from money he amassed

SCALE 1:29412 or about 2¼ INCHES to 1 MILE 3.4CM to 1KM

during the Hundred Years War with France, it was partially demolished and left in ruins after the Civil Wars in the 17th century, but fortunately restored and made habitable again in the 19th. It has a pleasantly irregular appearance, dominated by the Portmare Tower and the ruined, but nevertheless most impressive, Banqueting Hall. Sudeley Castle played an important role in the turbulent political struggles of the 16th century and is particularly well known because of its associations

with Catherine Parr, the sixth and last wife of Henry VIII, who came to live here, died here and is buried in the 15th-century church close to the castle.

Return along the drive and follow it through the park. Go through a gate by the side of a lodge **J** and keep ahead along the road, cross over the river and make your way back to the starting point in Winchcombe. ●

Cleeve Common

Start	Cleeve Common
Distance	8 miles (12.75km)
Approximate time	4 hours
Parking	Stockwell Common parking and picnic area (if full, other parking areas nearby)
Refreshments	None
Ordnance Survey maps	Landranger 163 (Cheltenham & Cirencester) and Pathfinders 1066, SO 82/92 (Cheltenham) and 1067, SP 02/12 (Stow-on-the-Wold)

Two statistics help to explain Cleeve Common's popularity with walkers: it is the largest remaining area of unenclosed 'high wold' and it includes the highest point in the Cotswolds (1083ft/330m). Many rights of way cross it, but these are largely irrelevant, as public footpaths are no clearer than other tracks and this is common land so walkers can wander freely. Golf balls can be a hazard, however, as much of the western part is occupied by a golf course. The views are extensive, and the prehistoric burial chamber of Belas Knap is a bonus to a particularly scenic and interesting walk.

The fine view looking westwards from the car park over Tewkesbury and the Vale of Gloucester is a mere appetiser for what is to come. From the car park walk down the main road for a few yards and at a public footpath sign, opposite a bus shelter and telephone-box, turn left over a stile to begin the ascent of Cleeve Hill. Bear slightly right and head steeply uphill – there are many paths, passing disused and now grassed-over quarries, across part of the golf-course and through a prehistoric circular enclosure, The Ring, making for a marker-post and just beyond that a toposcope and triangulation pillar **Ⓐ**.

The magnificent 360° view from here, one of the finest in the area, includes Cheltenham, Gloucester, Tewkesbury, the Vale of Severn, the mountains of South Wales, the Malverns, Bredon Hill and a large slice of the Cotswolds.

At the triangulation pillar turn right and follow a line of marker-posts across the common between the greens and bunkers – an 'up and down' route which keeps along the edge of the escarpment, past the rocky cliff of Cleeve Cloud and with superb views across the vale all the way. Prehistoric earthworks litter the common and some of them have been utilised as features of the golf-course, as at Cleeve Cloud. Past the end of the course the path turns left and heads towards the radio masts in front, still

keeping along the edge of the escarpment, later by a wall on the right. From the masts **B** the highest point on the common – though not particularly outstanding – is marked by a triangulation pillar just ahead but here the route turns half-left away from the wall towards clumps of gorse. Then it bears half-right along a wide, straight, grassy path, heading gently downhill through rough grass and gorse to a metal gate on the edge of the common.

Go through and walk along the right-hand edge of a field, by a wall on the right, later continuing between fields downhill to Wontley Farm. At the farm buildings turn left along a track which ascends, bears right and continues along the left-hand edge of fields, by a wire fence and later a wall on the left. After passing between an avenue of hedges, turn right at a public footpath sign saying 'Belas Knap, Humblebee,

Winchcombe' on to a narrow path that keeps along the left-hand edge of a field, by a hedge on the left, heading straight for Belas Knap in front.

Climb a stone stile to reach the Neolithic long barrow **C**, 178ft (54m) long and probably the most impressive of the burial chambers found in the Cotswolds and the Severn valley. It was constructed around 3000 BC and when first excavated around the middle of the 19th century four separate chambers were discovered, containing the remains of over thirty human beings. A curious feature is the false entrance at the north end – was it built to fool potential tomb robbers or to ward off evil spirits? The restored drystone walling indicates that methods of constructing such walls have remained largely unchanged for nearly 5000 years.

Pass to the left of the burial chamber, climb another stone stile, turn left through a kissing-gate and continue along the right-hand edge of a field, by woodland on the right. At this point

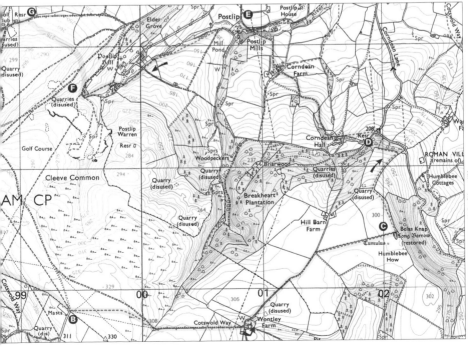

there is a fine view to the left of Cleeve Common. At the end of the field bear right to go through a kissing-gate and continue downhill, by a wall on the right, along the edge of the next field, following the field edge round to the left at the bottom end. Turn right through another kissing-gate and head down through trees to a road.

Turn left for a few yards until you reach a T-junction **D**. Climb up some steps which are directly opposite, climb over a stone stile at a public footpath sign to Postlip and bear left across a field down to a stile in a fence. Climb over and continue across the field, bearing left to go through a gate. Walk along a track, by a wall and a wire fence on the left, pass through a gate ahead and then continue along a broad grassy path in front of Corndean Hall, keeping to the left of a pond. Continue by a wire fence on the right, climb over a stile and walk along a path which curves gradually around to the left. Climb over another stile and bear right at a yellow arrow along the right-hand edge of a field, by a hedge and trees on the right. Go through a metal gate, walk past some farm buildings on the right and along a track, turning left to follow the edge of the field and continuing through Postlip Mill, a paper mill which is mainly modern but nevertheless still retains some of its earlier buildings.

The Vale of Severn from Cleeve Common

Bear slightly left along an uphill drive, turn sharp left **E** downhill along another drive and continue uphill again, turning right through the mill car park and passing through a yellow-arrowed gate at the far end. Continue along a track and where it bears left through a gate keep ahead along an overgrown path, battling through jungle but soon turning left over a footbridge across the River Isbourne. Now turn right along the edge of a field, by a hedge on the right, to a stile. Climb over and continue along the right-hand edge of the next field, climbing two stiles in quick succession and continuing along a narrow path, with a wire fence on the left and trees on the right, to a drive. Cross over, go through a metal gate opposite and keep ahead, by the boundary wall of Postlip Hall on the right, to go through a gate. Continue, still by the wall on the right, through two more gates, passing stables on the left, and walk uphill to go through another gate. Here the wall curves to the right but you turn left through a gate and head slightly uphill to another gate. Pass through and walk across a field towards the trees in front, continuing along a path through the trees and heading up to climb a stile which readmits you to Cleeve Common.

Turn right along the common's edge for a few yards and then bear left **F** uphill in a straight line, following a series of marker-posts over the shoulder of the common. Over the brow, head downhill towards the golf clubhouse in a straight line, avoiding golf balls again, to join a broad track **G**. Turn left and follow it along the edge of the common, passing the clubhouse on the right and continuing to where you rejoin the outward route. Here turn right over a stile to return to the road almost opposite Stockwell Common parking area. ●

Bourton-on-the-Water, the Slaughters and Naunton

Start	Bourton-on-the-Water
Distance	10 miles (16km)
Approximate time	5 hours
Parking	Bourton-on-the-Water
Refreshments	Pubs and cafés at Bourton-on-the-Water, hotel at Lower Slaughter, pub at Naunton
Ordnance Survey maps	Landranger 163 (Cheltenham & Cirencester) and Pathfinder 1067, SP 02/12 (Winchcombe and Stow-on-the-Wold)

One of the attractions of this lengthy walk is that it includes four villages that in varied ways rank among the most appealing in the Cotswolds: bustling Bourton-on-the-Water, idyllic Lower Slaughter, tranquil Upper Slaughter and tucked-away Naunton. A bonus is that the countryside around complements the villages, revealing a Cotswold landscape at its finest and most typical, with sheltered valleys of the rivers Eye and Windrush, pleasant woodland and expansive views across rolling country from breezy uplands.

It is easy to see why Bourton-on-the-Water is such a popular tourist spot. Lovely stone buildings line the wide main street through which flows the River Windrush, bordered by trees and lawns and crossed by a number of low bridges. Then there is a bird sanctuary, the Cotswold Motor Museum and, behind the Old New Inn, the Model Village – an exact replica of Bourton, $1/9$-size of the original. The parish church is a mixture of styles – medieval, Georgian and Victorian –and is characterised by an unusual dome on the rebuilt 18th-century west tower.

Start by walking along the High Street towards the church, turning right through the churchyard gates, passing in front of the church tower and continuing along a tarmac, hedge-lined path to a road. Turn left along the road up to the A429 and turn right. After about 100 yds (92m), turn left through a gate **A** at a footpath sign to Lower Slaughter and take the path ahead across a field to a gate. Go through that and continue along the tarmac path, bearing slightly right to join a hedge on the right, and on through another gate. Continue between hedges and later trees, by a stream on the left, into the village of Lower Slaughter **B**.

Considerably less commercialised, Lower Slaughter rivals Bourton, with its exquisite composition of fine old houses and cottages with the little River Eye between them, attractive stone bridges and tree-lined greens. The Victorian church was built in 1867. Turn left up the road to follow the river through the village, bear slightly left at a road junction in the direction signposted to Upper Slaughter, and continue by the river on the left, bearing right to pass to the right of the much-photographed mill.

Just past the mill buildings turn left along a path lined by walls and hedges, go through a kissing-gate a few yards ahead and continue through another one by a public footpath sign. Keep ahead along a grassy path, with the river on the left, later bearing slightly right away from it to go through a gate. Continue across a field, bear slightly right to go through a gate by a yellow waymark and continue across the next field to another gate at the far end. Go through and on between trees, dropping down to go through a gate by a stream. Cross the stream and keep ahead along a narrow tree-lined path into Upper Slaughter.

This is much more sleepy than Lower Slaughter, less obviously picturesque, but still a superbly attractive and unspoilt village of cottages grouped around a green. It has two manor houses, one a fine Elizabethan building and the other a former parsonage, now a hotel. As at Lower Slaughter, the church is mostly Victorian but retains some of its original Norman features.

Turn left along the road through the village, bearing right at the first junction **C** and turning left by a wooden seat, to continue along a track above the river on the right. The track descends and continues by the tree-lined river to a gate. Go through and follow the clear path ahead gently uphill to go through another gate and continue, by a hedge on the right, to a gate by a cottage. Pass through that and keep along a path through woodland above the river on the right, later descending to the river and following it along to a lane **D**.

Turn left and after ¼ mile (400m) just before the lane curves slightly to

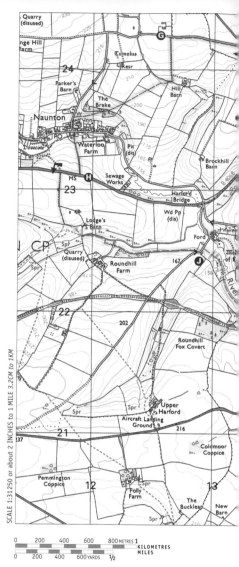

the left you see two broad tracks on the right. Turn right **E** along the second, past the end of a row of cottages, go through a metal gate and keep ahead, bearing slightly left and climbing gently by a wall, half-hidden at times by trees and bushes, on the left. Pass through a metal gate at the top and continue in a straight line over a series of fields through a succession of metal gates. After passing a barn go through another gate and turn left, following a broad track along the left-hand edge of a field down to a gate and a road **F**.

Cross over this, go through a gate opposite and at a bridleway sign to Naunton turn right along the edge of a field, by a fence and hedge and parallel to the road on the right. Bear left, still along the edge of the field, to a gate. Go through, cross a farm track, continue through the gate opposite and on along the field edge, through another gate and straight ahead to come out on to the road at a gap in the wall on the right **G**. Immediately turn left, at a public bridleway sign, down a broad track along the left-hand edge of a field, gently descending into the Windrush valley. At a junction of tracks keep straight ahead, following

bridleway signs, down to the bottom edge of the field and continue along a narrow path through trees, bearing right and heading up a slight rise. Continue across the middle of two fields, then across a third field, heading downhill towards a line of trees. At the edge of the field continue down through the trees to pass through a gate. With a fine view of Naunton in the valley on the left, keep ahead along a grassy path to a gate, go through and turn left down the lane into the village to a T-junction.

The medieval church and main part of the village are to the right; the Black Horse pub is just a few yards to the left.

Cottages by the River Eye at Lower Slaughter

At the T-junction take the track almost directly opposite, crossing the Windrush and passing through a gate. Keep along a grassy uphill path, between fences and with a small plantation on the right, to go through a metal gate and continue up to a wooden gate and metal kissing-gate side by side. Go through either and keep ahead along the edge of the next field, ascending gently to a road **H**. Turn right along the road, and at a public bridleway sign turn left through a metal gate along a broad track that keeps by the edge of a field, by a wall on the left. Head down to a stile, climb over and continue over the next field, bearing left and heading downhill to a metal gate with a blue waymark in the bottom corner, just over a brook. Go through the gate and keep ahead, parallel to the brook on the left, to a stile. Climb over and continue through the shallow valley, with trees both sides, to go through a gate. Keep ahead to go through another gate and continue for about 50 yds (46m) to a gate and lane **J**.

Cross over, climb a stile immediately opposite and continue ahead, soon joining the banks of the river on the left. Now follow a path across delightful riverside meadows, passing over a succession of stiles and through a number of gates. Later climb through gorse bushes above the river and bear right, by the right-hand edge of thick woodland, before entering the woodland, then heading straight across a field towards Aston Farm. Continue through the farm buildings and along a broad track to where it bends right. Here bear left along a path between hedge-banks, following it first as an embankment above fields both sides, and later across the middle of a large field, to emerge on to a tarmac track.

Turn left for a few yards towards a cottage and at a yellow waymark turn right through a metal gate and along the path ahead – this is likely to be overgrown – across an area of rough pasture. If the grass is long the path will not be visible but head down the slope towards the far end of the field, where it narrows almost to a point, to reach a gate and stile. Go through or climb over and continue straight across the next field, between a line of conifers on the right and the tree-lined banks of the river on the left, to a stile at the far end. Climb over and keep ahead along a path, looking for a gate on the right which leads on to the main road just to the left of a fork **K**. Turn left along the road, cross the river and turn right into a road called Lansdown, following the left bank of the placid Windrush back into the centre of Bourton-on-the-Water.

An attractive alternative finale is to turn right **L**, at a public footpath sign, on entering the village and walk along a path between a wall on the left and line of trees on the right to rejoin the river-bank. Soon turn right over a footbridge and then turn left along the opposite bank of the river. Pass through a gate and keep ahead, finally bearing slightly right away from the river to go through a kissing-gate and along a path between houses to a road. Turn left back to the village centre. ●

Chedworth and Withington

Start	Disused airfield about 1 mile (1.5km) north-west of Chedworth. Turn off Chedworth – Withington road along road to Compton Abdale and park about ¼ mile (400m) along by a right-hand bend
Distance	9 miles (14.5km)
Approximate time	5 hours
Parking	Plenty of parking spaces beside road through disused airfield
Refreshments	Pub at Chedworth, pub at Withington
Ordnance Survey maps	Landranger 163 (Cheltenham & Cirencester) and Pathfinder 1090, SP 01/11 (Northleach & Andoversford)

A large proportion of this walk is through the extensive woodlands, mainly of beech and oak, that clothe much of the country between Chedworth and Withington on the western slopes of the Coln valley. In the middle of these woods, occupying a platform above the valley, is one of the most complete Roman villas in England. This villa and the villages of Chedworth and Withington are the three focal points of the walk. There is much to enjoy: fine scenery and pleasant woodland as well as the two outstandingly attractive villages – both with interesting churches and hospitable inns – and the historic appeal of the Roman villa.

Start by taking the track that leads off from the road at the right-hand bend, by a public footpath sign, and in front of a metal gate turn right along a narrow path enclosed by wire fences, to a stile. Climb over, now leaving the airfield, and turn left along a path that keeps by the edge of Withington Woods on the right. Climb a stile and continue, turning left over another stile and right along the edge of a field, climbing another stile to come on to a road.

Cross over and take the track opposite, just slightly to the right, going through a metal gate and continuing along the edge of the woods, soon passing a house on the left. About ¼ mile (400m) further on you come to a clearing. Here turn right **A** along an obvious broad track and follow it through the delightful Withington Woods, keeping a sharp look out for the indispensable yellow waymarks. The route keeps mostly in a straight line, though at one stage it curves right and then left, later turning right in front of a group of fine old trees, following yellow waymarks all the time. Soon after that be careful: the main track bears left but you keep ahead along a narrower, quite overgrown path – look out for a yellow waymark – descending gently to a stile at the edge of the woods. From here there is a grand view ahead across the fields to Withington. Climb over the stile and bear left down to a yellow waymark in a gap in the hedge. Continue downhill across the next field, passing close to an electricity pylon, to another yellow waymark on a stile in a hedge. Climb over and continue diagonally downhill across the next field to the bottom right-hand corner, continuing for a few yards through bushes to climb a stile on to a road **B**. Bear left into the village, taking the first turning on the right to a T-junction.

Withington is a delightful village, its houses sloping down from the church to the Mill Inn by the bridge over the Coln. The church, a cruciform building described by William Cobbett in 1826 as 'like a small cathedral', dates mainly from the 13th century but retains two fine Norman doorways.

At the junction turn right downhill through the village, over the river and continue uphill, taking the first turning on the right, Woodbridge Lane **C**. Keep along this winding undulating lane, later joining the River Coln on the right, for ¾ mile (1.25km). At a footpath sign turn left **D** under a disused railway bridge, following a track round to the right for a few yards and then turning left over a stile at a yellow waymark. Continue along the bottom edge of sloping fields, slowly bearing right, below a ridge on the left and above the winding river on the right, to reach a stile half-hidden by trees. Climb over and following yellow marker-posts continue uphill, later keeping along the right-hand edge of a field. At the end of the field turn right over a stile and head downhill along the left-hand edge of a field, by a hedge and wire fence on the left. Climb a stile and continue, now by a wire fence on the right, to cross a footbridge over the

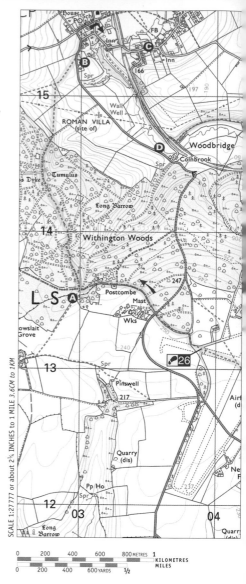

SCALE 1:27777 or about 2¼ INCHES to 1 MILE 3.6CM to 1KM

Coln. Keep ahead, bearing left to pass through a gate. Turn half-right and head uphill across a field, turning sharply to the right on meeting a sunken green path and following it up to a stile in the top corner.

Climb over and turn sharp left along a lane, on the line of an old Roman road called the White Way, following it downhill to a junction **E**. Here turn even more sharply to the right to follow a winding lane for 1 mile (1.5km) through the lovely Coln valley. At a

'National Trust Roman Villa' sign **F** turn right if you wish to visit the villa.

Chadworth Roman Villa, the finest of a number of villas in the Cotswolds, is in a lovely position, surrounded on three sides by woodland and overlooking the gentle, peaceful valley of the River Coln. As usual the Romans chose a good site: on the sunny sheltered slopes of the valley and close to a water supply. The villa was built in the early 2nd century and subsequently enlarged, most of the present remains dating from the 4th century. It comprised over 60 rooms, and contains bath suites, some fine mosaics and the remains of hypocausts, by which it was heated. Now owned and protected by the National Trust, there is an interesting museum on the site and an audio-visual display which explains the history of the villa.

Return to **F** and turn right (keep ahead where the lane bends left if not visiting the villa) along a track, at a sign saying 'Private Road, Footpath Only', that keeps by the edge of Chadworth Woods on the right. After 1 1/4 miles (2km) go through a gate and along the lane ahead for a few yards before turning right up some steps **G** to a stile; this is quite difficult to spot.

Climb over to enter Chedworth Woods and keep along a narrow uphill path, crossing one track and then bearing slightly right to join a second track. After a few yards, just before the track starts to curve to the right, turn half-left and head down to the wide stony track easily visible below. Bear right along it to continue through this most attractive stretch of mixed woodland.

On reaching the edge of the wood bear half left along a clear broad path across the field ahead, turning right, in front of two trees, along another broad path and heading in a straight line to a stone stile in a wall. Climb over and continue across the next field, then along the left-hand edge of the field after that, by a hedge on the left. At the far end turn left through a metal gate and walk along the right-hand edge of a field, by a wall and later a wire fence on the right, soon heading downhill and bearing right to a gate. To the right there are superb views of Chedworth village, its houses clinging to the steep hillsides. Go through the gate and turn right down a lane **H** into the village, climbing up from the valley bottom to the Seven Tuns pub **J**.

Unlike many Cotswold villages, Chedworth is spread out over a large area and its cottages and houses climb up the sides of the steep and narrow valley in an apparently random manner. It is a quiet off-the-beaten-track place but at one time the railway line from Cheltenham to Cirencester ran through it and a viaduct spanned the valley. This has now gone but the embankments are still clearly visible. The church, which retains some of its original Norman work but dates mainly from the thirteenth to the 15th century, overlooks the village from an elevated position at its north end.

Opposite the pub turn right past cottages up to the church. Go into the churchyard and passing the church on the right climb up some steps, by a wall on the left, and over a stile. Continue uphill, making for a stone stile in the wall ahead, climb it and walk along a tree-lined path, joining the parallel drive on the right to pass through a gate and on to a lane **K**. Turn immediately right along a broad track, climb a stile and continue along the track – at first walled both sides, later by a wall and wire fence on the right – to go through a metal gate.

Now you have to negotiate a piece of rather untidy country, the disused airfield – though derelict hangars and crumbling runways may be of interest to some. Route-finding can be a little difficult here, as parts of the airfield have been cultivated; the former runways are probably the best landmarks. Bear half-right across grass, passing to the right of old airfield buildings, to join a runway where it bends to the right. Continue in the same direction across a cultivated area to a junction of four runways. Bear left along one of these and climb a stile to return to the starting point. ●

Withington Church

The Rollright Stones

Start	Long Compton
Distance	9 miles (14.5km) Shorter version 8 miles (12.75km)
Approximate time	4½ hours (4 hours for shorter version)
Parking	Layby to north of Long Compton
Refreshments	Pubs at Long Compton, café at Wyatts Farm shop, ¼ mile (400m) south-west of point **H**
Ordnance Survey maps	Landranger 151 (Stratford-upon-Avon) and Pathfinder 1044, SP 23/33 (Moreton-in-Marsh & Hook Norton)

A minor road runs along a ridge, which forms the Warwickshire-Oxfordshire border and was once part of a prehistoric trackway across the country. Along this ridge are the Rollright Stones, a group of Bronze Age remains which form the focal point of this lengthy and quite demanding and hilly walk. From Long Compton the route climbs via field paths on to the ridge, drops down the other side to the tiny hamlet of Little Rollright and climbs back up to the Rollright Stones. It then continues along the ridge to the village of Great Rollright, before descending for the final leg back to Long Compton. The route can be shortened by omitting Little Rollright.

Long Compton is aptly named: the village straggles for over a mile (1.5km) along the Stratford-upon-Avon to Oxford road. It is an attractive place, the main street lined with honey-coloured thatched and stone houses and cottages. The imposing church is approached by an unusual two-storeyed, timber-framed lych-gate, possibly once a cottage.

Start by walking south through the village, passing the church on the right, and just after Butlers Lane on the left turn right **A** through a gate beside a large house on the left and walk along a grassy path for a few yards to another gate. Go through, turn half-left and head across a field. Go through a gate in a wooden fence ahead and continue over the next field – there is no obvious path – to go through a metal gate. Keep ahead a few yards to join a broad track that keeps

along the right-hand edge of a field, by a hedge on the right, and soon starts to ascend the ridge ahead. After the hedge on the right ends, the path continues uphill across a field, veering slightly left towards a stile in the top left-hand corner.

Climb it and still keeping in the same direction head diagonally uphill across the next field, making towards a hedge on the right and a metal gate in the top right-hand corner. Go through, continue across the next field towards the farm in front, and just before the farm buildings follow the hedge on the right as it curves to the right, passing through a gate. Continue past the right-hand edge of the farm buildings and keeping roughly in the same direction head straight across the middle of the next field, making for the right-hand edge of the trees on the horizon. Climb a stile at the top end of the

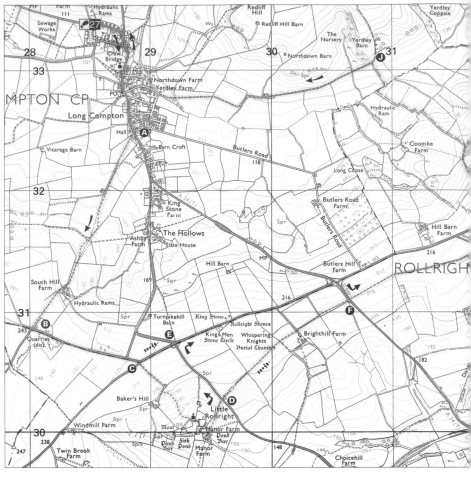

field and turn left along a road **B**. Keep along this for ¹/₂ mile (800m) and just past the turning on the left to Long Compton and Shipston there is a T-junction **C**.

*At this point the walk can be slightly shortened by turning left and omitting Little Rollright, rejoining the route at **E**.*

Go through the metal gate opposite, at a footpath sign to Little Rollright, and walk along a broad farm track heading downhill. By some barns on the left the track turns right, but you keep ahead through a gap in the hedge and continue downhill across the middle of a field towards Little Rollright church. At the bottom end of the field continue along a track, passing the church on the left,

down into the hamlet which comprises little more than a few cottages, farms, a manor house and a simple and small mainly 15th-century church.

Just after the track bends left turn left, at a footpath sign, along a grassy path by some old barns and sheds on the left, and at a yellow waymark continue straight across a field to another yellow waymark in a hedge, beyond which is a lane **D**.

*Here you can continue straight ahead along a waymarked route over fields to rejoin the route at **F**, to avoid some road walking – but by doing so you omit the Rollright Stones, the focus of the walk.*

To continue on the main route, turn left up the lane to a road junction and turn right **E** along the road which runs along the ridge, giving extensive views over both sides. A little way along is the group

of Bronze Age remains known as the Rollright Stones. These comprise three monuments: the King's Men, a circle of over 70 stones on the right, the isolated King's Stone on the left, and a little further on, also on the right, the Whispering Knights or Five Knights, a burial chamber.

Continue along the road, which follows the line of a prehistoric track, for $^1/_2$ mile (800m) to where it joins the main Stratford–Oxford road. Here turn right for a short distance, looking for concrete steps in the wooded embankment on the left . Climb these to a footpath sign for Great Rollright at the top and go along a path, between fields both sides, keeping more or less in a straight line. Eventually veer slightly to the left, between a hedge on the left and a line of trees on the right, to a gate and a lane. Go through and turn right along the lane for $^1/_4$ mile (400m) to a crossroads ⓖ.

Here detour to the right if you wish to visit Great Rollright. Otherwise, just before the crossroads, turn left at a bridleway sign beneath an avenue of trees to a gate a few yards ahead. Go through and continue along the right-hand edge of a field, by woodland on the right, following the field edge round to the left, keeping parallel to a road on the right and eventually turning right at a bridleway sign on to it ⓗ. (Turn left here if you wish to visit Wyatts Farm Shop café.)

Cross over, pass through a metal gate opposite, at a bridleway sign, and cross the field ahead, later joining and keeping by a hedge and wire fence on the right and heading downhill. Pass through a metal gate, turn right along a track for a few yards and bear left to go through another metal gate. Keep along the edge of the next field, by William's Copse on the right, go through a gate and turn left along the left-hand edge of the next field, by a wire fence and hedge on the left. Continue downhill along the left-hand edge of several fields to a gate.

Go through, bear left and walk along the left-hand edge of the next field, following a zigzag route but keeping by the line of trees and hedges on the left all the while. In the far corner follow the field edge round to the right for about 100 yds (92m) and then turn left into the trees. Go through a gate, cross a footbridge and continue along the edge of a field, by a hedge on the left, climbing to join a track ⓙ.

Turn left along this broad track and follow it across fields for the next $1^1/_2$ miles (2.5km), through several gates and over stiles, back to Long Compton, its church tower acting as a prominent landmark. On reaching the edge of the village, go through a metal gate and continue along a lane to the main road, turning right back to the starting point. ●

The King's Stone at Rollright

Bredon Hill

Start	Overbury
Distance	9½ miles (15.25km)
Approximate time	5 hours
Parking	By the church at Overbury
Refreshments	Pubs at Overbury, Ashton-under-Hill and Conderton
Ordnance Survey maps	Landranger 150 (Worcester & The Malverns), Explorer Map No. 14 (Malvern Hills and Bredon Hill)

In summertime on Bredon
The bells they sound so clear;
Round both the shires they ring them
In steeples far and near,
A happy noise to hear.

So wrote A.E. Housman, and certainly there can be few more pleasant places to be on a fine summer day than the summit of Bredon Hill. The bells that 'sound so clear' must refer to those in the churches in the many attractive villages that encircle the base of the hill, two of which are featured in the walk. This is the north-west frontier of the Cotswolds – Bredon's familiar outline is detached from the main range by the Vale of Evesham and overlooks the low-lying country watered by Shakespeare's Avon. The route falls naturally into two parts: the climb over the hill itself – lengthy but gradual and easy – and a walk across the fields at its foot.

Overbury is a tranquil and dignified village of stone and half-timbered buildings with an outstanding cruciform church, one of the few in the country to be dedicated to St Faith. Externally its main feature is the grand 15th-century tower but inside its great glory is the Norman nave, a rare survival in a village church.

Begin by the church and walk along the road towards Kemerton. Just past where the road bends slightly to the left, turn right **Ⓐ** through a wooden gate, then turn half-left and head diagonally across a field to go through a gate in the far corner. Continue along the edge

of two fields, with a hedge and wooden fence on the right, to pass through a gate and on to the road at Kemerton. Cross over and take the lane almost opposite, turning right at the first junction **Ⓑ**. Head uphill, passing modern houses and old cottages, and where the lane bends right go through a gate and along an uphill track. This is the start of the ascent of Bredon Hill.

The track climbs along the right-hand edge of two fields and at the end of the second field turn left, at a yellow waymark, along its top edge. From here there are grand views of both the Malverns and the Cotswolds. The path curves slightly left and then right and then, by a house on the left, go through a gate and ahead a few yards to a track **C**. Turn right on to this broad uphill track, at first beneath an avenue of trees and later continuing between hedges, taking the left-hand track at a fork. Continue climbing, between hedges and trees on the right and a wire fence on the left, turning left through a gate at a blue waymark. Continue along the top edge of a field for a few yards and then turn right along a broad hedge-lined track. A few yards downhill in the trees on the left are the King and Queen Stones, two rocky outcrops that throughout the ages have had healing properties attributed to them.

Continue along the uphill track, by a field on the right and a steep wooded bank on the left, and near the top bear right along a grassy path, by a wall and wire fence on the right, later skirting a small plantation on the right and passing through a gate at the end of it. Continue, still by a wall and wire fence on the right, but with the plantation now replaced by broad-leaved woodland. Turn right to go through a gate, by a bridleway sign at the top end of the field, into the narrow band of woodland, The Warren. Walk along the right-hand edge of this, by a wire fence on the right, curving through a beautiful tree-lined avenue to a gate. Go through this to leave the wood and then continue along the edge of a field, by a wall on the left, passing through another gate and on to Parsons Folly, the 18th-century tower that marks the summit of Bredon Hill (961ft/293m) **D**.

The magnificent views from here take in a large slice of the Midlands, and in clear conditions one can see as far as the Welsh mountains. It is not surprising that the summit was used as a fort in prehistoric times, and the earthworks of the Iron Age enclosure

can be still clearly identified, as can the Banbury Stone, another prominent outcrop that has become a focal point of legend and superstition.

Continue across the summit, keeping by the wall on the left as it curves round to the right. The villages of Great and Little Comberton can be seen to the north, as well as Pershore with its abbey tower. Go through a gate and keep along the edge of a small wood on the right, continuing, by a fence on the right, along the ridge with superb views ahead looking towards the Cotswold ridge and Evesham.

Now begins the descent. Head downhill to a gate at the edge of a wood, go through it and continue along the right hand edge of the Long Plantation, by a wire fence on the right, for just over 1 mile (1.5km), passing through a gate at the end of the plantation. Continue along the edge of fields, by a wall on the left, descending gently to go through a gate. Keep ahead, still by a wall on the left, bearing right to a bridleway post and Wychavon Way sign. Here turn left to go through a gate, descend between banks to a signpost and bear slightly right down to a metal gate.

Go through, bear half-left and head downhill across the field, looking for a waymarked stile in the hedge on the

The church at Overbury

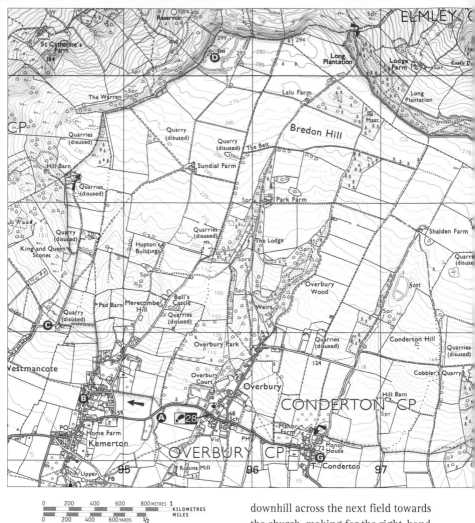

0   200   400   600   800 METRES 1
━━━━━━━━━━━━━━━━━━━ KILOMETRES
MILES
0   200   400   600 YARDS   ½

left. Climb over, continue downhill across the next field to climb another stile and keep in a straight line down to the next stile. Climb over that and follow the direction of the arrow straight across the middle of a particularly long field, passing two isolated trees, which are useful guides, to a signpost ahead. From here continue across the rest of the field, dropping quite steeply towards Ashton-under-Hill church which can be seen ahead. Cross a farm track by a signpost at the end of the long field and immediately climb two stiles ahead in quick succession. Bear slightly right downhill across the next field towards the church, making for the right-hand edge of a hedge and bearing left by the churchyard wall on the left, to a metal gate **E**.

If visiting Ashton-under-Hill, go through and keep ahead past the church into the very attractive village of stone and half-timbered thatched buildings. The church, like that at Overbury, is unusually fine for a village church and is also dedicated to a little-known female saint, St Barbara, patron saint of 'armourers and gunsmiths, firearms and fortifications'.

Otherwise, turn right in front of the gate along the bottom edge of the field you have just crossed, by a wire fence and pool – known as The Moat – on the

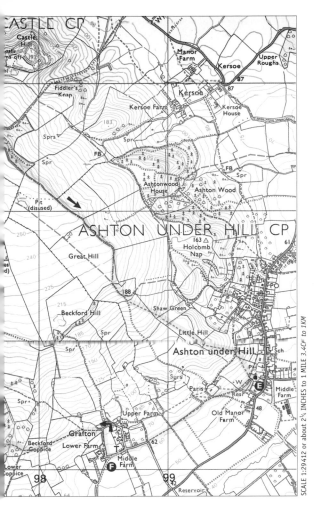

an almost hidden public footpath sign to Conderton, go through a gate, bear half-left and head across a large field.

The next part of the walk is quite tricky as there is no visible path, but head uphill, skirting the bottom edge of a field on the right, and continue straight across this large field to a wire fence and line of trees at its far end. Look out for a stile about 100 yds (92m) up from the bottom left-hand corner, climb over and head straight across the next field – again there is no path – towards the woods in front and a more obvious stile. Climb that and take a narrow but clear path through Beckford Coppice. Emerging from the trees cross a brook

left, to a metal gate. Go through, continue along the edge of the next field, climb a stile and turn right along a broad track, by a wire fence on the right. At a fork bear slightly left in front of a house on the right and keep along the right-hand edge of a field, soon joining a hedge on the right. At the end of the field cross a footbridge over a brook and head straight across the middle of the next field to go through a metal gate, just to the right of some cottages, and on to a lane.

Walk along the lane for ¼ mile (400m) turning right **F** on to a side lane by the side of Lower Farm and continuing between the houses and thatched cottages of the hamlet of Grafton to the end of the lane. Here, at

and bear slightly left to join a track which continues along the edge of a field, by a wire fence on the left.

Cross a track and continue along the edge of a field, by a hedge on the left. Keep along the edge of the next field, following it around as it bears right to a gate in the hedge on the left. Go through, and continue along the edge of a field, by a wire fence on the left. Climb over a stile and keep along the edge of the next field to climb another stile on to a lane a few yards ahead.

Turn left into Conderton village, smaller than either Ashton-under-Hill or Overbury, more of a hamlet. Turn right **G** along the road in front of the Yew Tree Inn and follow it for ½ mile (800m) back to Overbury. ●

Further Information

The National Trust

Anyone who likes visiting places of natural beauty and/or historic interest has cause to be grateful to the National Trust. Without it, many such places would probably have vanished by now.

It was in response to the pressures on the countryside posed by the relentless march of Victorian industrialisation that the trust was set up in 1895. Its founders, inspired by the common goals of protecting and conserving Britain's national heritage and widening public access to it, were Sir Robert Hunter, Octavia Hill and Canon Rawnsley: respectively a solicitor, a social reformer and a clergyman. The latter was particularly influential. As a canon of Carlisle Cathedral and vicar of Crosthwaite (near Keswick), he was concerned about threats to the Lake District and had already been active in protecting footpaths and promoting public access to open countryside. After the flooding of Thirlmere in 1879 to create a large reservoir, he became increasingly convinced that the only effective way to guarantee protection was outright ownership of land.

The purpose of the National Trust is to preserve areas of natural beauty and sites of historic interest by acquisition, holding them in trust for the nation and making them available for public access and enjoyment. Some of its properties have been acquired through purchase, but many have been donated. Nowadays it is not only one of the biggest landowners in the country, but also one of the most active conservation charities, protecting 581,113 acres (253,176 ha) of land, including 555 miles (892km) of coastline, and over 300 historic properties in England, Wales and Northern Ireland. (There is a separate National Trust for Scotland, which was set up in 1931.)

Furthermore, once a piece of land has come under National Trust ownership, it is difficult for its status to be altered. As a result of parliamentary legislation in 1907, the Trust was given the right to declare its property inalienable, so ensuring that in any subsequent dispute it can appeal directly to parliament.

As it works towards its dual aims of conserving areas of attractive countryside and encouraging greater public access (not easy to reconcile in this age of mass tourism), the Trust provides an excellent service for walkers by creating new concessionary paths and waymarked trails, maintaining stiles and foot bridges and combating the ever-increasing problem of footpath erosion.

For details of membership, contact the National Trust at the address on page 95.

The Ramblers' Association

No organisation works more actively to protect and extend the rights and interests of walkers in the countryside than the Ramblers' Association. Its aims are clear: to foster a greater knowledge, love and care of the countryside; to assist in the protection and enhancement of public rights of way and areas of natural beauty; to work for greater public access to the countryside; and to encourage more people to take up rambling as a healthy, recreational leisure activity.

It was founded in 1935 when, following the setting up of a National Council of Ramblers' Federation in 1931, a number of federations earlier formed in London, Manchester, the Midlands and elsewhere came together to create a more effective pressure group, to deal with such problems as the disappearance and obstruction of footpaths, the prevention of access to open mountain and moorland and increasing hostility from landowners. This was the era of the mass trespasses, when there were sometimes violent confrontations between ramblers and gamekeepers, especially on the moorlands of the Peak District.

Since then the Ramblers' Association has played an influential role in preserving and developing the national footpath network, supporting the creation of national parks and encouraging the designation and waymarking of long-distance routes.

Our freedom to walk in the countryside is precarious and requires constant vigilance. As well as the perennial problems of footpaths being illegally obstructed, disappearing through lack of use or extinguished by housing or road construction, new dangers can spring up at any time.

It is to meet such problems and dangers that the Ramblers' Association exists and represents the interests of all walkers. The address to write to for information on the Ramblers' Association and how to become a member is given on page 95.

Walkers and the Law

The average walker in a popular walking area, armed with the appropriate Ordnance Survey map, reinforced perhaps by a guidebook giving detailed walking instructions, is unlikely to run into legal difficulties, but it is useful to know something about the law relating to public rights of way. The right to walk over certain parts of the countryside has developed over a long period, and how such rights came into being is a complex subject, too lengthy to be discussed here. The following comments are intended simply as a helpful guide, backed up by the Countryside Access Charter, a concise summary of walkers' rights and obligations drawn up by the Countryside Commission.

Basically there are two main kinds of public rights of way: footpaths (for walkers only) and bridleways (for walkers, riders on horseback and pedal cyclists). Footpaths and bridleways are shown by broken green lines on Ordnance Survey Pathfinder and Outdoor Leisure maps and broken red lines on Landranger maps. There is also a third category, called byways: chiefly broad tracks (green lanes) or farm roads, which walkers, riders and cyclists have to share, usually only

Traitor's Ford

occasionally, with motor vehicles. Many of these public paths have been in existence for hundreds of years and some even originated as prehistoric trackways and have been in constant use for well over 2000 years. Ways known as RUPPs (roads used as public paths) still appear on some maps. The legal definition of such byways is ambiguous and they are gradually being reclassified as footpaths, bridleways or byways.

The term 'right of way' means exactly what it says. It gives right of passage over what, in the vast majority of cases, is private land, and you are required to keep to the line of the path and not stray on to the land on either side. If you inadvertently wander off the right of way – either because of faulty map-reading or because the route is not clearly indicated on the ground – you are technically trespassing and the wisest course is to ask the nearest available person (farmer or fellow walker) to direct you back to the correct route. There are stories about unpleasant confrontations between walkers and farmers at times, but in general most farmers are co-operative when responding to a genuine and polite request for assistance in route-finding.

Obstructions can sometimes be a problem and probably the most common of these is where a path across a field has been ploughed up. It is legal for a farmer to plough up a path provided that he restores it within two weeks, barring exceptionally bad weather. This does not always happen and here the walker is presented with a dilemma: to follow the line of the path, even if this inevitably means treading on crops, or to walk around the edge of the field. The latter course of action often seems the best but this means that you would be trespassing and not keeping to the exact line of the path. In the case of other obstructions which may block a path (illegal fences and locked gates etc), common sense has to

be used in order to negotiate them by the easiest method – detour or removal. You should only ever remove as much as is necessary to get through, and if you can easily go round the obstruction without causing any damage, then you should do so. If you have any problems negotiating rights of way, you should report the matter to the rights of way department of the relevant council, which will take action with the landowner concerned.

Apart from rights of way enshrined by law, there are a number of other paths available to walkers. Permissive or concessionary paths have been created where a landowner has given permission for the public to use a particular route across his land. The main problem with these is that, as they have been granted as a concession, there is no legal right to use them and therefore they can be extinguished at any time. In practice, many of these concessionary routes have been established on land owned either by large public bodies such as the Forestry Commission, or by a private one, such as the National Trust, and as these mainly encourage walkers to use their paths, they are unlikely to be closed unless a change of ownership occurs.

Walkers also have free access to country parks (except where requested to keep away from certain areas for ecological reasons, eg. wildlife protection, woodland regeneration, safeguarding of rare plants etc), canal towpaths and most beaches. By custom, though not by right, you are generally free to walk across the open and uncultivated higher land of mountain, moorland and fell, but this varies from area to area and from one season to another – grouse moors, for example, will be out of bounds during the breeding and shooting seasons and some open areas are used as Ministry of Defence firing ranges, for which reason access will be restricted. In some areas the situation has been clarified as a result of 'access agreements' between

Countryside Access Charter

Your rights of way are:

- public footpaths – on foot only. Sometimes waymarked in yellow
- bridleways – on foot, horseback and pedal cycle. Sometimes waymarked in blue
- byways (usually old roads), most 'roads used as public paths' and, of course, public roads – all traffic has the right of way

Use maps, signs and waymarks to check rights of way. Ordnance Survey Pathfinder and Landranger maps show most public rights of way

On rights of way you can:

- take a pram, pushchair or wheelchair if practicable
- take a dog (on a lead or under close control)
- take a short route round an illegal obstruction or remove it sufficiently to get past

You have a right to go for recreation to:

- public parks and open spaces – on foot
- most commons near older towns and cities – on foot and sometimes on horseback
- private land where the owner has a formal agreement with the local authority

In addition you can use the following by local or established custom or consent, but ask for advice if you are unsure:

- many areas of open country, such as moorland, fell and coastal areas, especially those in the care of the National Trust, and some commons
- some woods and forests, especially those owned by the Forestry Commission
- country parks and picnic sites
- most beaches
- canal towpaths
- some private paths and tracks Consent sometimes extends to horse-riding and cycling

For your information:

- county councils and London boroughs maintain and record rights of way, and register commons
- obstructions, dangerous animals, harassment and misleading signs on rights of way are illegal and you should report them to the county council
- paths across fields can be ploughed, but must normally be reinstated within two weeks
- landowners can require you to leave land to which you have no right of access
- motor vehicles are normally permitted only on roads, byways and some 'roads used as public paths'

the landowners and either the county council or the national park authority, which clearly define when and where you can walk over such open country.

Walking Safety

Although the reasonably gentle countryside that is the subject of this book offers no real dangers to walkers at any time of the year, it is still advisable to take sensible precautions and follow certain well-tried guidelines.

Always take with you both warm and waterproof clothing and sufficient food and drink. Wear suitable footwear, ie. strong walking boots or shoes that

give a good grip over stony ground, on slippery slopes and in muddy conditions. Try to obtain a local weather forecast and bear it in mind before you start. Do not be afraid to abandon your proposed route and return to your starting point in the event of a sudden and unexpected deterioration in the weather.

All the walks described in this book will be safe to do, given due care and respect, even during the winter. Indeed, a crisp, fine winter day often provides perfect walking conditions, with firm ground underfoot and a clarity unique to this time of the year.

The most difficult hazard likely to be encountered is mud, especially when

Further Information

walking along woodland and field paths, farm tracks and bridleways – the latter in particular can often get churned up by cyclists and horses. In summer, an additional difficulty may be narrow and overgrown paths, particularly along the edges of cultivated fields. Neither should constitute a major problem provided that the appropriate footwear is worn.

■ The Cotswold Voluntary Warden Service

The Cotswold Voluntary Warden Service was formed in 1968 in order to assist in the preservation and promotion of the Cotswolds Area of Outstanding Natural Beauty.

The principal objectives of the Warden Service are: to provide facilities which improve public access and enjoyment of the countryside; to promote the qualities of the countryside, thereby enhancing the public's appreciation of them; and to protect the countryside from excessive, potentially damaging use.

The service is administered by Gloucestershire County Council. Further information can be obtained from:

View towards Painswick

Cotswold Warden Office, County Planning Department, Shire Hall, Gloucester GL1 2TN
Tel. 01452 452674

■ Follow the Country Code

Enjoy the countryside and respect its life and work
Guard against all risk of fire
Take your litter home
Fasten all gates
Help to keep all water clean
Keep your dogs under control
Protect wildlife, plants and trees
Keep to public paths across farmland
Take special care on country roads
Leave livestock, crops and machinery alone
Make no unnecessary noise
Use gates and stiles to cross fences, hedges and walls
Reproduced by permission of the Countryside Commission

■ Useful Organisations

Council for the Protection of Rural England
Warwick House, 25 Buckingham Palace Road, London SW1W 0PP
Tel. 0171 976 6433

Countryside Commission
John Dower House, Crescent Place,
Cheltenham, Gloucestershire GL50 3RA
Tel. 01242 521381

Forestry Commission
Information Department,
231 Corstorphine Road, Edinburgh
EH12 7AT.
Tel. 0131 334 0303

Long Distance Walkers' Association
21 Upcroft, Windsor,
Berkshire SL4 3NH
Tel. 01753 866685

National Trust
Membership and general enquiries:
PO Box 39, Bromley, Kent BR1 3XL
Tel. 0181 315 1111

Ordnance Survey
Romsey Road, Maybush, Southampton
SO16 4GU
Tel. 08456 05 05 05 (Lo-call)

Ramblers' Association
1/5 Wandsworth Road, London SW8 2XX
Tel. 0171 582 6878

Heart of England Tourist Board
Woodside, Larkhill Road,
Worcester WR5 2EF
Tel. 01905 763436
Local tourist information offices:
Abingdon: 01235 522711
Bath: 01225 462831
Broadway: 01386 852937
Burford: 01993 823558
Cheltenham: 01242 522878
Chipping Norton: 01608 644379
Cirencester: 01285 654180
Evesham: 01386 446944
Gloucester: 01452 421188
Newent: 01531 822145
Northleach: 01451 860715
Stroud: 01453 765768
Witney: 01993 775802
Woodstock: 01993 811038

Youth Hostels Association
Trevelyan House, 8 St Stephen's Hill,
St Albans, Hertfordshire AL1 2DY
Tel. 01727 855215

 Ordnance Survey Maps of the Cotswolds

The Cotswolds are covered by Ordnance Survey 1:50 000 (1¼ inches to 1 mile or 2cm to 1km) scale Landranger map sheets 150, 151, 162, 163, 164, 172 and 173. These all-purpose maps are packed with information to help you explore the area. Viewpoints, picnic sites, places of interest and caravan and camping sites are shown, as well as public rights-of-way information such as footpaths and bridleways.

To examine the Cotswolds in more detail, and especially if you are planning walks, Ordnance Survey Pathfinder maps at 1:25 000 (2½ inches to 1 mile or 4cm to 1km) scale are ideal.

Maps covering this area are:

1020 (SP 04/14)	1092 (SP 41/51)
1021 (SP 24/34)	1113 (SO 80/90)
1043 (SP 03/13)	1114 (SP 00/10)
1044 (SP 23/33)	1132 (ST 69/79)
1066 (SO 82/92)	1133 (ST 89/99)
1067 (SP 02/12)	1151 (ST 68/78)
1068 (SP 22/32)	1152 (ST 88/98)
1089 (SO 81/91)	1167 (ST 67/77)
1090 (SP 01/11)	1168 (ST 87/97)
1091 (SP 21/31)	1183 (ST 66/76)

Explorer Map No. 14 (Malvern Hills and Bredon Hill) covers part of the Vale of Evesham and the Cotswold Outlier Bredon Hill. Tourists will also find the Touring Map of the Cotswolds, Map No. 8, useful as it helps them to make the most of their stay.

To get to the Cotswolds, use the Ordnance Survey Great Britain Routeplanner Travelmaster map number 1 at 1:625 000 (1 inch to 10 miles or 1cm to 6.25km) scale.

The Ordnance Survey Travelmaster Guide *Cotswolds Car Tours* features 20 car tours with coloured mapping and details of places of interest, colour photographs as well as useful addresses for further local information.

Ordnance Survey maps and guides are available from most booksellers, stationers and newsagents.

Further Information

Index

Entries in italics refer to illustrations